SOME THOUGHTS ON SOCIAL RESPONSIBILITY

Revised Edition

William D. Eldridge, Ph.D.
The Ohio State University

UNIVERSITY PRESS OF AMERICA

Lanham • New York • London

University Press of America,® Inc.
4720 Boston Way
Lanham, Maryland 20706

3 Henrietta Street
London WC2E 8LU England

Printed in the United States of America
British Cataloging in Publication Information Available

Library of Congress Cataloging-in-Publication Data

Eldridge, William D.
Some thoughts on social responsibility /
William D. Eldridge. — Rev. ed.
p. cm.
1. Social ethics. 2. Responsibility. I. Title.
HM216.E38 1994 303.3'72—dc20 93-48775 CIP

ISBN 0-8191-9431-X (cloth : alk. paper)
ISBN 0-8191-9432-8 (pbk. : alk. paper)

The paper used in this publication meets the minimum requirements of American National Standard for Information Sciences—Permanence of Paper for Printed Library Materials, ANSI Z39.48-1984.

CONTENTS

Chapter I

UNDERSTANDING THE "BASICS" OF HUMAN GROWTH AND DEVELOPMENT

Everything that happens throughout life's excursion is entwined within the basic "code" or blueprint of human developmental dynamics. Our destinies are fashioned, therefore, by the following:

1. Fundamental characteristics of the organic "machine," house and support the energetic "productive" life force. We call this force symbolic thought (differentiated from animal instincts), the "heart," our soul, God's light-incarnate, the "essence" of being, etc.

2. Neuro-physiologic "electricity" represents metaphorical "thought images," which are stored in memory as internal re-creations of external "realities." We perceive them through stimulus-differentiating sensory nerves of taste, touch, hearing, sight and smell.

3. "Learned" formulas of psychosocial adaptation are retained by childhood conscious and unconscious survival-seeking minds. They are a prescription for (a) negotiating rewarding relationships with parent-figures, and (b) integrating individual needs with cultural rules, values and opportunities.

4. There is (a) a fundamental pattern of accelerated growth through adolescence, (b) lengthy "stabilized maturation" and equilibrating balance through young to middle adulthood, (c) progressive "deterioration" toward old age, and (d) an immediate, unpredictable "moment" of system discontinuance, at death.

Unfortunately, life scenarios and "ideational" *content* of personal and culturally programmed thoughts and associated confirmational behaviors, *totally dominate* awareness. They occupy our thinking time: "I think—I act in accordance with these unseen mental images, my behaviors are observable—therefore there must be a 'me' [a composite self] which possesses some form of relevant existence." We seldom reflect on primordial or elementary aspects of ontologic (being) existence and epistemologic "ways" of knowing (as opposed to facts or "things" we know). The failure of humanity to look honestly and critically at "itself," results in *outcomes of perceiving and behaving* which accomplish these negative functions:

1. We create lack of unity between the parts of *our* selves and symbolic image-producing functions. These are bifurcated into components of mind which (a) think the original thought (pure electricity) and (b) watch the first part doing the thinking and (c) define this neurologic moment as an integrated "whole" with the rest of our physical being (the identity).

2. We prevent ourselves from "feeling" sameness with "other" people, leading to exaggerated beliefs of differentness. This causes fear and antagonistic competition for physical and ideological resources for survival.

3. We create belief systems of truth, beauty and value (axiology) which (a) represent illusions or delusions of life's meaning, in order to (b) control fears of vulnerability/failure/death—but which (c) result in depression or despair when we realize they are pretend "sand castles of relevancy." These structures are created by a being with alternate choices for using mental capacities, which do not necessarily have discrepancies between what we "are," and what we want to "be."

Given the above representations of "truths" about "authentic" dimensions of life, it is refreshing to take a step backward, to consider the initial and continuing "status" of the life form we call homo sapiens. This provides an existential mirror, where "rungs of life's ladder" can be viewed relative to one another, and understood as *dependent* and predetermined aspects of the antecedent "whole" which emerged at birth.

Premature Birth

Many physiologists and anthropologists tell us that the large circumference of the human head, which contains a substantial brain for symbolic thought and creative reasoning, predisposes us to early nativity, relative to other mammalian species. Our maternal host's vaginal expansion cannot accommodate a longer intra-uterine period of prenatal maturation, during which the head would grow too large to permit successful birth. Humans use sophisticated processes of sensory data collection from the environment, cognitive analysis of symbolic ideas, and complex memory procedures, for considerable extra-uterine "learning" and experiential orientation. These operations do not seem to be required of "lower" life forms, which rely on instinct, rather than reasoning, for physical survival. Humans, therefore, appear to need an earlier birth timetable, so that maturational development emerges in an "interpreting" organism within a "stimulating" environment. This seems different from "other" animal species whose survival capacities for food, water, body temperature control, rest and shelter are pre-programmed in genetic codes. These blueprints produce "automatic" processes for need-satisfaction (shedding cycles for body covering, relationships between natural predators and prey, hibernational patterns, flight responses to fearful stimuli, etc.), relative to evolutionary "priorities" of ecologic-environmental supply and demand.

We are born, therefore, with considerable "potential" for progressive adaptational "analysis" of the environment. This includes integration of behaviors to manipulate objects, with mental "plans" for arrangement of events in sequence to increase survival probabilities (i.e., buy sneakers to run fast, catch the bear, start a fire, then have dinner, etc.). We have, however, little encoded natural "sense" about the confusing world-at-large, so humans undergo extensive dependent tutelage with superordinate parent-figures who "show us the ropes." The human is not equipped with (or has evolutionally lost) sufficient genetically engineered decision-making "impulses" to shorten the infancy learning stage, and survive independently with "functional" behaviors. Extended childhood development, therefore, "authorizes" expanded environmental opportunities for independent or interdependent action. These options are characterized by (1) superior levels of power (manipulative "tool using" alteration of natural resources); (2) creative potentials to coordinate activities with constant and variant environmental contingencies; and (3) ability to symbolize "realities" with "logical" reasoning to control future occurrences, understand the past, and apply value weightings to internal or external "happenings."

Basic Needs

In early childhood, we learn in ways similar to animal relatives, through modeled behaviors which *produce* pleasurable sensations, and *avoid* painful outcomes. This represents association of "natural" consequences (hot stove, uncomfortable body postures, etc.) and "social" exigencies for successful survival (silence around guests, putting toys away, avoidance of public masturbation). In social situations, outcomes represent artificial and subjective aversions for frequently confused neophytes (spanking, hand-slapping, parent frowning and yelling, bodily removal from "desirable" physical location, etc.). Consequences are often experienced as physical "abuse" (punishment) prior to the child's development of reasoning ability. Initial contact with the world involves physical contingencies of pleasure and pain, with food ingestion/elimination, temperature control, rest, postural comfort, and avoidance of excessive light and sound stimuli as predominant focal points. When maturation unfolds, we use coordinated body, sensory, and thinking capacities to meet physical survival needs—but these "animalistic" drives become progressively easy to satisfy, and blend into broader frameworks of psychic and social living. Our conscious minds forget their focal centrality, but frustrations and previously experienced "deprivations" are remembered within "unconscious" "anchoring" ideologies. Many recollected "traumas" of insufficient or delayed need-satisfactions continue to drive motivations and adult behaviors.

Need Elaboration

Physical survival "appears" to diminish as a primary adaptational goal or crisis, through increasing competencies of the child, to "operate" on the world to achieve satisfying "sensually-perceived" existence. The thinking/reasoning/abstracting juvenile therefore, discovers an expansive social and spiritual/aesthetic environmental panorama. Physical survival needs have been symbolically enhanced, appended, and comprehensively transformed into a myriad of social and psychological "superordinate" or overarching "needs." Each of course, must be energetically fulfilled (or defensively denied/repressed) throughout each person's physical life (spiritual post-mortem life will be discussed later), as dictated by norms of cultures, and the dreams and opportunities of individual citizens thereof. The creative image-producing mind has "embellished" each basic need with a range of hierarchically valued and qualitatively discriminated subsets of correlated thoughts and behaviors. In the mind of the still dependent youngster, these become separate "domains" of reality and truth. Each possesses significance, as *associated* dimensions of "subsistence" requirements, but also takes on its own "life form" and stimulus force of attractiveness and meaning. Reality is organized as singular conceptual "units" of existence within external culture, and internal psycho-emotional components of the "self." In a pragmatic and *structural* way, need-meeting activities are accoutered with a supplemental array of *artifacts,* behavioral *rituals,* or sensory *stimuli* (e.g., food ingestion becomes a "meal" with elaborated utensils, decorative surroundings, visual [T.V.] and/or auditory stimulation [soft music], and aesthetically differentiated food items). As a result, original survival behavior becomes disguised or perceptually *transfigured* as something "beyond" itself. In fact, however, eating is just eating to stay alive, regardless of packaging or mental "decoration" that is attached. The same structural pseudo-alteration occurs, obviously, for each survival behavior (i.e., fashionable clothes, water-beds, recreational relaxation, concordant colors and music to "soothe the savage beast," etc.). These all become "principles, processes, poignancies, and premiums" to be learned and re-articulated within each family and culture of world inhabitants.

From a *functionalist* perspective, elaboration of physical need-meeting acts into a labyrinth of substituted objects, events, customs, and social rituals, has three results:

1. Extended appendages of baseline survival serve as "time and space fillers" to keep us busy. Technology creates leisure opportunities during which the primitive, "electrical impulse" part of our minds simply rests and does little productive work. Meanwhile, image-building and self-observing "mentations" notice that the absence of developmental thought (building blocks between idea symbolizations), leaves the human "machine" in a dormant state of nothingness and "irrelevance."

2. Extensions, in the form of external objects of possession or appreciation, support the "notion" that thought and memory interact to form an holistic and "relevant" self, with variegated degrees of psycho-emotional "need." These needs are stimulated and satisfied by sensory interaction with a paired set of known and not-yet-discovered external artifacts, which are visible symbols of the complex inner self.

3. Elaboration of external realities into comparatively valued goals and objectives, functions to nurture some aspects of the human bio-physical system. This system metabolizes and regenerates itself through cardio-vascular and neuro-muscular activity, produced and supported by increases in electrical synaptic functions of the brain.

Human Dependency

As children observe associations of subsistence needs with elaborated extension artifacts/objects, they also "learn" that *pleasurable* sensations (e.g., gentle rocking in cradled arms) and amelioration of *pain* (warm milk in stomach) are *directly* linked to a human "service provider." "Emotional feeling," emerges and functions intricately with the earliest parent-child associational "bondings." These begin with the mother's identification of "self" in the "security-producing reflection" of relevant and "concretized" existence. As the fetus is nurtured ("part of me, creating another part of me, which will ultimately validate my existence and meaning in life"), emotion "materializes" as the child realizes its excessive vulnerability. She or he "converts" traumatic painful physical sensations into counter-balancing physical energies of combined discomfort and excitation (stimulative anticipation of need-satisfaction). This energy is paired with psychosocial "value or significance quotients" (memory traces/ideas) that add "overload anxiety energies," as *loss* and return-to-physical *pain* status are continually recollected. Internal conditions of interchange between remembered statuses of satisfaction and deprivation are symbolized (given external benchmarks) in facial or body expressions, variations in vocal sounds, and language configurations. The developing child imitates and later uses these criterial references as need-identifying signals to manipulate nurturing behaviors from caregivers.

Choreographed communications between parents and children "convince" the latter that their "identity" (a self composed of non-observable "ideas" attached to physical events or objects) is intimately "united" with some other life form. The "adequacy" of this maturing self-image (internal electrical impulses made real by associating external phenomena to parallel "assumed" personality "parts") is "causally" linked *and* existentially "validated" within the context of physical, and emotional *relationships,* assuming the following "perceived" characteristics:

1. Internal "conditions" of the child's organism, manifest through external body and verbal "language," are assumed to have linear (direct and sequential) stimulus and response "creational" and "constitutional" *connection with the host* parent. The child, in many ways, believes the two personalities share some form of post-partum "oneness."

2. Pleasurable organic "states" (or absence of displeasure/pain) are elaborated into psychic levels of a "pleasured" (valuable, relevant, successful, loved, needed, etc.) self-concept. Various qualitative "positions" or psycho-emotional places of differential "significance," are assumed to be contingent on *evaluations* of behavioral manifestations. These externalities, in turn, represent (re-present) unseen aspects of self which are emitted "non-cybernetically" (e.g., child *causes* parent evaluation which, in turn, "proves" the child exists in the defined state, *but* parents' pre-existing agenda does not cause the evaluation and produce a false diagnosis of the child's "ontology" [nature or condition of being], nor does the parent cause the child's reaction, which then causes the reciprocating evaluation).

3. Achievement of equilibrium (metabolic equivalence between energy expended and energy saved or nutritionally consumed) demands *alteration* (e.g., return to attitudinal "baseline" prior to parental negative evaluation) of *parents'* internal *state* of pleasure/pain ratio. This condition is represented as a "real" equivalent emotional state via symbolic external semaphoric messages. It is also seen in the child's reinforcement of

continuations of parental positive demeanors through additional expenditures of neuro-psychophysical energy.

4. The degree of parental control and need-satisfying/depriving manipulative capacity observed by the vulnerable child, leads to assumptions of reality "permanency" and fear-reducing identity consistency. Subsequently, this illusion translates into the young person's "mirage" of a "solid state" personality to match their material physique. A concrete, integrated, boundaried, incarnate "self" becomes either a positive or negative foundation to further define its past, present or future emerging thoughts and actions. It also becomes a static comparative standard against which we measure similarities or differences with other "identities."

5. The collaboration of developing logic with the "fine-tuning" of sensory receptors in a "spongelike" maturing organism, causes the child to "put 2 and 2 together" in a fixed formula of decision-making. This formula (a) emerges quickly, but not creatively, to bring ideologic "unity" to otherwise chaotic existence, and (b) parallels decisioning patterns of parents who are emulated through role modeling and, reinforce values and thought patterns which reflect their own likenesses.

"Higher" Level Needs

As school age and adolescent development emerge, bio-nutritional/energetic/equilibrium "survival" considerations disappear from *direct* focus. Escalating exposure to community, peer and other interpersonal situations introduces an expanding "stage" of emotional survival needs. These substitute for "approval" contingencies experienced by the "consolidating self" in the nuclear family atmosphere. The young person remembers connective linkages between physical pleasure and parental personality. They organize an irrational conglomerate of sensory data from the world "out there," into a system of related mental "images" and systematized action procedures (verb tenses to "reason-out" influential relations between concepts). Collections of images consolidate into an "illusion" of a metaphysical or emotional "self" which actually exists in corporate electro-sensory reality. Children believe this collection of "machine-operations" actually constitutes an architecture-like "whole-corpus" which is a repository for a hierarchy of autonomous needs. The pacification of this engorged set of "deprivations" is then "differentiated" socially, into three branches of goal-directed effort, which function as follows:

1. Gradations of symbolized "currency income" reward various behaviorally manifested thought productions. Rewards enable satisfaction of expanding

higher level "aesthetic desires" through ownership of qualitative/quantitative material "symbols" of survival. These are increasingly (until older age sets in) interpreted as control over primitive ecological environments. They are also seen as a kind of "profit-value" (a la Marxian capitalism) relative to social preference or quality of workmanship (hours of effort or time of production), or economic exchange value (e.g., quality furniture, precision musical orchestration, etc.).

2. Positive sentiment from other people affirms the "self" we possess, and replicates some standardized "ideal configuration" of coordinated thoughts and behaviors. The self is validated as "goodness or acceptability" relative to expectations of others, secondary to a formula for their *own* possession.

3. Capability for "independent" thoughts (in concert with stress increasing or reducing behaviors) reduces anxiety relative to perceptions of need-deficit. They also increase stimulation, to artificially transport levels of emotional existence to higher positions of valued "actualization, appreciation, insight, or fulfillment."

This brings us to ideology, and the nature of thought and conception, as an integral part of developmental process. At the beginning of life, although every child's brain manifests electrical activity, the predominant "anchoring" mechanism to connect "blank pages" of the personality to a world of images, symbols, ideas and physical objects—is the visual system of light reception on the retina. "Messages" from the external world "attack" the unsuspecting infant through other sensory organs, and their "responses" and manipulations become organized, consistent and goal-directed as sight (substitute "imaging" process for blind individuals) provides initial concrete symbols of a reality "out there." The child mentally "converts" sensations and energies into a *representational* set of "world-equivalent" *units of imagery and truth* inside their own heads. As each fixes attention on various objects (including parenting figures) in our immediate environment, the "nature" (shape, texture, color, etc.) of these units of reality is transmitted via differentiated particles of light rays, through comprehensive matrix waves and movement patterns. Patterns are received by photo receptive cells in the posterior eye, and are transformed into discriminating electrical impulses. They are then registered in sophisticated neuro-sensory cellular tissues that retain the image in structurally modified, but representationally parallel, symbolic form. For example, light reflects a red automobile, but this "reality," as we conceptualize it, is essentially light waves, electrical currents, cerebral fluids, and cellular tissue. This energy picture registers a phenomenologic imprint instantaneously, at which point, almost simultaneously, the brain moves on to the next sensory input. Presence of the next event alters homeostatic patterns of light/sound/chemical substance environments that interact with our sensory receptors.

For the child, accumulation of neurologic symbols includes stationary images of objects or events which simply "are." Also, another set of awarenesses registers combinations of object representations which are "associated" through application of physical energy, applied by a human "bridging link." As the mind develops intricate sets of associations between distinctive external objects (patterned collectivities of highly mobile atoms, with "seemingly solid" forms), the child views the world as a matrix or puzzle which:

1. appears to "fit together" with an overall integrated and "meaningful" scenario which *can be discovered* by searching for the "right" explanatory and constructive formula;

2. can be controlled, owned, mastered or manipulated through the use of tools and physical effort;

3. is characterized by a continuous "flow" or unified ensemble of events and themes, and is "represented" by synthesized blends of analytic and organizational symbolic thoughts;

4. constitutes a "purposeful" system of cause and effect contingencies, with "logical and functional outcomes" that can be understood with human reasoning;

5. probably has increasing "relevance" as an arena whereupon "emotional and spiritual natures" of humankind are evaluated relative to "quality" of expression;

6. represents phenomena which appear contradictory, anomalous, irrational, destructive, etc.; and which can be removed from disturbing consciousness by accepting "dependence" on a superior controlling "persona" or force which (a) possesses an overarching rationale for reality, and (b) hosts some system of exchange value whereby "benefits" can be "earned."

Ideology

Growing children develop capacities to create, interchange, combine, and diversify mental symbols to represent "domains" of physical and metaphysical "existences." They are perpetually reminded, shocked, or nudged herein, into confronting "gaps" or contradictions in the otherwise "smooth, coherent, and positive" journey of life. The *first,* remembered pungently in the darkened recesses of the mind's unconscious, is that we are a highly *vulnerable and fragile organism.* Although achieving monumental intellectual and emotional latitudes of existence, we *fundamentally and ultimately* are controlled by needs for food, frequent sleep, temperature and stimulation control, and connectedness with similar life forms. We realize that physical "beginning" leads to "ending," that growth and deterioration exist side-by-side, and there is simultaneous presence of pleasure and pain (joy and sorrow, feast and famine) which appears logically contradictory.

A *second* "light bulb" flashes when we hear reports from marketing surveys, voting predictions, attitude polls, consumer profiles, sociologic studies, or historical "trend" analyses. This "awareness" reacquaints us with patterned, *conditioned, collective* and the culture/group-*dependent nature* of what we ironically define as adult "independence." Profound attachment to external controls is exemplified by the following: (a) persistence of childhood emotional conflicts which no longer "relate" to adult reality (and seem "irrational" or unexplainable), (b) sustenance of parents' values into substrata of our contemporary thoughts and behaviors, plus (c) concomitance of "personal" activities and viewpoints which are identical, to hundreds of thousands of other "free" people.

Point number *three* relates to the previous issue, and is an unresolvable tug-of-war between "perceived" opposite polarities of independence vs. dependence. Cultural paradigm shifts, relationships between people and organizations, as well as neurotic debates in our minds, elucidate human *ambivalence* about the true and most desirable "state of the psychic being." This pendulum of personal and cultural preference swings back and forth with its incessant search for the "right" combination of allegiances to "self" or "other." This resolution is supposed to insure a more "meaningful" present, or prepare us for a qualitatively differentiated future—of ending or beginning.

The *fourth* gap in understanding our "situation" occurs during moments of philosophical or spiritual reflection. We observe (or think we observe) our presence in a micro *and* mega-massive "system" of shared space and survival interdependencies (we eat other animals and plants, but what eats us besides cancer cells and ulcers?) with other life forces (sun, wind, water, magnetic fields, gravity, etc.). Given the assumption of a supreme creator, being, or force, we want to believe there is a "point" to all of "this." "Functional" relationships to other ecological "energies or being-forms," however, appear circumscribed in a redundant pattern of staying-alive-in-order-to-stay-alive. We try to die-later-rather-than-sooner, as though death is "differentiated" by time. In more optimistic visions of what "is," we contemplate origins or outer boundaries of the universe, but become perplexed in understanding the why, where, when, how or even what of existence. Agnostic or atheistic viewpoints also create frustration, where prima facie "cause or intent" is less relevant, but human emotions, creativity, and passions for living dominate the explanatory spotlight. These are accompanied by various skepticisms about "accidental" causes of monumentally complex life support systems (e.g., human cardiovascular network, plant growth and sustenance, etc.).

The *final* point involves a less frequently experienced, yet frightening and perplexing awareness, which relates to existentialism, and phenomenology, which observe and explain processes of generating ideas, psychic awarenesses, and cognitions. When mental activity (electrical brain wave modulations) is viewed as a purely physical or neurologic occurrence, this "animation" appears a relatively continuous process, which tells us "we exist." If another classificatory lens is used, however, to view thought and define conscious manifestation of distinct imagery symbols, then there appear to be discernable "empty spaces" between singular units of cognition. These are noticed during states of "mindless" or "ego-less" meditation, and during periods of stress or loneliness, when minds have difficulty engaging in ritualized or accustomed stimulus-response repertoires of mental focus. The rapidity of the mental "computer," gives the illusion of a continuous stream of consciousness, which begs the question of whether we "are," only when we conceive of an "it."

In the above examples, belief, value, explanation, etc. play a significant developmental role, especially as symbol-transporting "vehicles":

1. Ideology and value fill gaps between unexplainable polarities in observed and sensed experience.

2. Ideology and value supply cause and effect formulas where "nature's dynamics of operation" are beyond or obscured from logic of reason.

3. Energy of ideologizing (the "zing" is what happens here) occupies time and space between segments of direct thought electrical activity.

4. Ideology and value constitute diagnostic or categorical "criteria" which (a) organizes incoming stimuli into differential subsets, and hierarchies of relational "significance," (b) assigns values to symbols of external reality, along with attachment of mental representations of influential and manipulative energy, and (c) internalizes a large world into a smaller cognitive "scale model" which we "rearrange" to gain beliefs of control.

5. Ideology and value provide an overarching "system of relevancy" by which observable and metaphysical/spiritual phenomena are conceptualized with singular or associational attributes of "potency" or conclusive testimonial "efficacy." This signifies the validity, functional importance, and

productive value of personal or cultural goals and objectives of thought, feeling and action.

Personal or social belief systems are fortified with fresh foci and devotional energy during personal crises or national/worldwide "revitalization" movements. These centering episodes represent perceptions of individual or collective "explanatory" minds which are cornered or trapped. This occurs with overwhelming evidence (from unconscious awareness or external conscious experiences), of diametrically contradictory "facts" (e.g., life and death, goodness and badness, independence and dependence, infinite and finite, Coke and Pepsi, etc.) which cannot be "rationally" blended into a unified mural of life. Existential "holes in reasoning" are filled semipermanently with interconnecting esoteric "principles and truths" of life. These become (or appear to become) concretized during periods of individual or collective history when they are utilized. In this context, they produce beliefs of a unified "whole" life scenario where pain, effort, work, loss, joy, accomplishment, possession, differentiation, etc. all "make sense" relative to a functional beginning, middle and end "plot."

With "ideology-creating" ability, however, to (1) deal with "vulnerability" of the human "condition," plus (2) supply "meaning" where it does not automatically emanate from sensory experience (to "ice our own cakes"); the reader may ask why we should give *any* substantive analytical consideration to "growth and development" as a topic of *social responsibility*. To answer this question, the following subsection outlines ways in which "psyches" utilize, misinterpret, overindulge, ignore, destructively translate, or delusionally falsify various components of human essence we can "know" empirically and pragmatically. Processes of skewed knowing, additionally, produce *alienation, pain,* and *displeasure* in the "self" or other "selves" as we search for need-satisfaction. Growth and development, as it unfolds, is not the problem, therefore, but heterogeneity of "subjective" response to our observations of "us growing," becomes a psychological and social concern of great magnitude.

Destructive Interpretations of Human Development

All of us develop a relatively standardized set of dynamic functions, through a series of stages, to learn (1) basic trust in ourselves and others, (2) autonomy and self-control, (3) sexual and emotional attachment and detachment, (4) industriousness and personal/social achievement, (5) interpersonal intimacy, (6) social responsibility, and (7) psychological balance and resolution of conflicting emotions. Unfortunately, "natural" aspects of cognitive and physiological development serve as reinforcing public symbols and confirming metaphysical justifications, of the "correctness and wisdom" of cultural norms and values.

They are interpreted and given meaning by social role models (parents, peers, authority figures, community leaders, heroes/heroines, relatives, etc.) who communicate in subtle, ironic, disguised, inadvertent, reversed or direct ways—all "truths" of life. These "validities" have served, in *their* minds and experience, as the cornerstones of *their* adaptive existence. There are basic problems, however, with socialization or personal idiosyncratic acquisition of prescriptive verities:

1. "Teachers" of truth have a subjective interpretation.

2. Sociocultural patterns change slowly, so "what" is taught during childhood periods of learning may be outdated when applied later.

3. Most people are comfortable modeling "answers" (assumed facts) rather than "questions" (non-facts or alternate facts).

4. Completing stages of development is often traumatic, so "facts and feelings" (knowledge of self and knowledge of non-self external objects) become confused.

5. Values are inculcated, modeled, rewarded (deviance punished), at an early age, when decision-making, and evaluative and integrational skills are incapable of understanding and "personally indexing" validity, relevancy, or application of "principles." The child does not have the power or opportunity to assert "human rights" contingencies relative to involuntary and subordinate "learner roles."

6. Learning is accompanied by physical reward, punishment, deprivation, or indulgence, so options to "not learn" certain facts, behaviors, or attitudes are rarely adjusted to the unique receptive or need hierarchies of the child. What is learned is manipulated by parents, teachers or other authorities who control "survival" options for "inferior" junior persons.

7. Relearning at later ages is possible, but difficult, regarding foundation ideologies or heritage value tapestries. Most social and work roles narrowly focus domains of attention and belief, and maintain equilibrium (homeostatic stability and continuation), through reduction of substantive inputs of "new basic truths."

With these cautions in mind, I now want to discuss major arenas of social "irresponsibility" and psychological "irrationality" which emanate from participation in our *own* development process. Irresponsibility contributes to pain, alienation, guilt, fear and other forms of discomfort in our "mind's relationship to itself," and in associations with others.

Incorrect Identity Formulas we Establish

Definition: Identity formulas are systems of relationship between *thought content* we are "expected," or *have* learned, to generate regularly on cue (e.g., "Dad's democratic views are correct"), or avoid. They represent "logical" *sequences of reasoning* which we believe will produce "correct" deductions and adaptive actions (e.g., "Hard work will *always* make me adapt, keep me safe, reduce anxiety, etc.; I am a hard worker, therefore I will succeed"). Identity formulas represent *states of "being"* to which we are "entitled," representing fixed or valued conditions of existence ("I am basically 'bad' but might possibly achieve some goodness"). They constitute beliefs about *motivations of others* which can be "predicted consistently" ("Men can't be trusted to be loyal"). They are *"energy" potentials* of our own thoughts or actions (creative and manipulable "futures") to influence outcomes of events, behavior/ideas of others, or internal states of self-esteem.

Causes: The overwhelming *influence* on idiosyncratic, family-normative or culturally ethnocentric "beliefs" about (1) *who* we are, (2) *how* we got that way, (3) *what* "powers" manage our lives, and (4) *which* options we possess for future "identities"; *centers* on the critical relationship between the following:

1. Humans exemplify extreme vulnerability during long periods of "primate" dependency on parental nurturance.

2. Humans have essential "emptiness of mind" and corresponding absence of "instincts" for short or long-term environmental adaptation.

3. Humans evidence capacity of brain and neuro-sensory systems to gather vast amounts of "input" in the form of "perceptual images," and instantaneously "learn" representational meanings.

4. Humans show the need and ability to "store" large quantities of information. We struggle with influential characteristics of this "unconscious file cabinet" to validate, cumulatively build, and apply "significant" information learned *early* and at specifically *critical developmental periods* of information-deficit/need "crises." A confounding characteristic is the neuro-structural "boundary" between conscious and unconscious mental processes which frequently prevents learned "facts and formulas" from being changed by more accurate newly-acquired "awarenesses."

The scenario, then, goes like this: (1) we are helpless for a long time in childhood, (2) we "bond" with "superior" caretakers to meet needs and assuage fear/anxiety, (3) we learn vast amounts of parent-generated "truth" which we "swallow and remember whole," (4) our minds are "spongelike storage bins" but are unable (early on) to make logical decisions about this "mandated socialization," (5) we emerge into a family or community environment which reinforces parents' beliefs about what "is," and (6) new information is "indexed" in accord with what we already "know." So, we do not experience "cognitive dissonance," which places us in "existential crisis" of having to explain why we previously (and presently) behaved in ways which were *false*. If former beliefs are judged to be incorrect, we question what proof we have that current "realities in our interpretive minds" are not equally distorted.

Problems: Life marches on, and we carry value-laden "formulas of being," which infant-child-adolescent-young adult maturation substantiates in self-confirming "identities." We may not be aware of *encumbrances* which this formula (truth—with a "logical and assumed" coherent syllogism of epistemology-knowledge development) instills in our personalities. Although some, or all, interpretations of "problem jacquards" may not be "quality of living" issues for each reader, some conflict-free behaviors with which *we* are homogenized, may represent obstacles to self-actualization *for others* with whom we relate. The following are examples of identity formulas, represented as "humanistic" problems in ideologic frameworks, which can be deleterious to both self *and* others:

1. *"I'm bad"*—There are numerous themes of diminished self-concept, but results are similar, whereby the "self-conceiver" experiences varying doses of auto-induced psychic pain. This results from incorrect assumptions of the power of parental or social "opinion" to *define* "being status." "Badness" is reinforced through a learned reconciliation *formula* which specifies that the "self" can only become "good" (or good again) by working industriously to *change* the *evaluation* of the "defining" agent. The irresponsibility of this illusion of a "state of the organism" (composed of blood, tissue, electricity, air and water—so what is this "self" anyway?) is that the holder of this "I'm bad" idea robs the rest of society of *their* creative knowledge or energy. We tie up time, money and effort of people/social agencies that "therapize" us, etc., whom we reduce into the "please approve of me" game. Yet, we resent and reject them for having control over our lives, and consequently insure we always lose a little, rather than risking bigger loss of "all the marbles" we envision down the road. Although each earthly dweller has the right to be miserable forever, there is a serious question

of self-imposed "authorization" to bear and rear involuntarily created children who must model or overcome this stigmata. There is also concern about our right to subject other adults to the defensive insults of manipulative communications, which the "bad" person inevitably uses to cushion harmful blows they strike against themselves. These come as (a) lies and seductions to create dependency, (b) projective criticisms of the character of others, (c) rejections of others' attempts to establish intimacy, and (d) excessive expectations of children or other adults to "live up to standards" we never achieve.

2. *"I'm Good"*—Although counselors, authors of "self-help" books, etc., find little objection to "positive" self-concepts, there are intricately veiled deceptions which transmogrify a self-actualizing personal image, into a socially and individually irresponsible "role-set." The problem with "good," as an anchoring adjectival perception, is that part of its identity derives from comparative inversion of the concept "bad," or the progression of "good-better-best." This suggests a *formula* by which one does or does not attain this "status." In the case of "learned" prescriptions, acquisition of the "good" label represents conformity to socially sanctioned "targeted" attitudes or behaviors. These, detrimentally, may not parallel individualized "expression" of each person's "self," as it is compared to its *own* "conditions of existence," or juxtaposed to other independently selected "criteria of adequacy." The "true" self may differ from traditional cultural "norms" of desired nepotistic self-indulgence concerning society's constituencies.

Where a "bene-coexistential" status is "conferred," rather than "earned," there is the philosophical question of rationale for "differentiation" itself, when the following conditions exist: (a) the creator of the status (e.g., God, life forces) already knows the condition of being we occupy and does not need to "call it" anything; (b) there is no necessity for us to "know" what we "are" and "cannot not be" it (why assert the inevitable?); (c) being in a position to "earn" status (relative to a priori "falling from Grace,") means returning to a "pre-morbid" condition where we are "good enough" to not know we are "bad" (or conversely "good" for that matter), so why not, not be good in the beginning. A final question is why we must achieve "goodness" *relative* to worldly righteous adaptation, where we (1) return to dependency in dealing with "selective truths" perpetrated by a vulnerable social order, or (2) are forced to juggle a complicated triadic allegiance to [a] the creator, the [b] "self" as a reflection of the creating essence (value, purpose, function, etc.), and [c] other createes.

Given complications of all of the above, "goodness" role *irresponsibilities* are noted as follows:

a. *We prematurely accept "full" self-actualization* when additional growth ("not yet good enough") might provide greater life satisfaction (note: this "personality roulette," becomes a delusional game of gambling for parental approval rather than accepting its irrelevancy to completion of the self).

b. We *obsess with the process* of earning goodness, with concomitant illusions that the personality actually "becomes" anything other than it already "is." We should question whether "verbs" of thinking or doing actually influence "nouns" of thinking-that-we-are-"being." This poses the dilemma of understanding how pure cognition (electrical brain waves) can be separated into "doing" and "being" subcomponents.

c. *Self-righteous control of other identities* seems "useful," where satisfaction with our own secure psychosocial haven predisposes "truth-articulating" interactions, which control their behavior. This facade results in anxiety conflicts among children, or produces narrowly channeled peer associations which fall short of "full plumage" to which they might aspire.

d. We adopt *symbolically masked vulnerability* ("badness") whereby we discriminate against, and prejudge others of "lesser" quality. Alienation ushers in repercussions, as negatively defined "minorities" or "deviants" fight back one way or another to regain human dignity (e.g., abusing welfare "charity," disrespect for property and majority rights, open revolt, passive-aggressive irresponsibility in "subordinate" work roles, etc.). There are additional psychic "costs" to *us* of maintaining *distance,* despite human need for connection (we may all have started from just two parents—animal, mineral, or vegetable).

3. *"I'm a Consumer"*—The cognitive formula to perpetuate a self-image, whereby conceived internal "ego-materiality" (functional "identity") subsumes a relationship with external or intramural stimuli, can be a problem as follows: (a) we see the "self" recurrently in a "need-deprivation" condition (less than "whole"); (b) this "state of the self" is considered "normal" and can be changed/enhanced/valuated most effectively by "reception" of external "stimulation"; (c) external events are "authorized" relative to capacity of consumers to transform and

"use" extrinsic energy to "add to" or fulfill the "self-minus-something"; and, (d) anxiety is generated when roles are reversed and we feel compelled to "supply" the needed psycho-commodities for other people. This "self" was "overindulged" by parents who expected minimal reciprocity in giving, and receiving, or was deprived of "demand-stimulated" nurturance. Life becomes a "recapitulative" search for the elusive satisfaction and comfort which the body "truly" needed in infancy, and the mind "believes" it needs transubstantially throughout adulthood.

Approaching life as a *consumer* (as opposed to a "producer,") contributes several *questions* of "qualitative" living. These interface with psychosocial hypotheses of "responsibility" to the universal "essences" (common denominators of transhuman existence) of the "life-energy" we share with others:

a. Can the "consuming personality" relieve self-perceived emotional "pain" when others need leadership rather than followership from them?

b. Can any of us experience anxiety-free balance and unification of the demanding bipolarities of the cognitively-constituted self, if one "hemis-persona," or domain, dominates the existential field of awareness and action?

c. Can uni-directional energy flow ever satisfy the conflicted, reconstituted dependent child's "need" for autonomy, which evolves as a consequence of (1) culturally learned aspirations for independent "creative" thought, and (2) anger emanating from lengthy childhood constraints on bio-psychic proclivities for maturational "expansion" (energy to maintain chemical metabolic homeostasis plus cognitive self-actualization in gaining mastery over invasions of sensory stimuli)?

d. Can "consumer" profiles of culturally stratified groups (e.g., welfare recipients, jet-set socialites, etc.) (1) become ecologically equilibriated to the extent that differentiated factions (i.e., rich vs. poor, where each group needs its opposite to validate its "self") (2) do not revolt (the poor attack authority and are destructively repelled—the rich attack each other and fall from the pinnacle) and (3) lose "something" in dealing with frustrations of blocked "productivity" and functional social contribution?

e. Will maturing children ever be free of constraining identity templates, which retard social progress or creative exploration? Herein, each generation replicates the previous "administration," then uses its energy to revolt—before even attempting new, autonomous, reality-based thought to fashion the future.

4. *"I'm Productive"*—This formula reverses the consumptive model, to the extent that "ideations" of adequacy are causally predicated on completing "work" or other goal-directed outcomes. This model suggests that human dependency represents compulsions to equate degrees of self-quality, with symbolized parallel gradations of "product" achievement. Of course, sequential levels of identity, "merit/distinction," etc., do not exist as *pure,* unalloyed "domains" of any synthesis of physiology, psychology and neurology. Differential statutes are, however, arbitrarily developed as cognitive "images" through comparative symmetry to physical phenomena. They are superimposed upon an "imaginary plane" of physical sensation, memory content, and behavioral patterns—to produce a security-confirming illusion of a safe "self." These articulated relevancies, then, are assigned cumulative extrapolative and interpolative linear "energy" dimensions, where past → present → future "accomplishments" are viewed in a collective and retrospective evaluative framework. This evaluation assigns current/future potential "status," and "predicts" anticipatory behaviors. A childhood game of guess-"what"-you-are-relative-to-parental-"standards"-of performance, may generate energy (relative to assumptions of the maladaptivity of the inert human organism which would evolutionally extinguish itself) to control an unyielding natural environment (i.e., grow food, secure warm clothing, etc.). It may in turn, however, not be fully "adaptive" when basic needs are easily satisfied technologically. This plan also dysfunctions when society decides upon "esoteric" aspects of "self-expression," which are only elaborations of bio-survival needs. Productivity orientations in this framework become "irresponsible" under the following circumstances:

a. Criteria for determining "competence" remain inflexible where changes in biologic capability or other life circumstances cannot be "integrated" into existing attributional values via indexed metamorphic conversion (e.g., running 1 mile at age 40 = 1/2 mile at age 60). They also cannot be abandoned for updated categories of personal adaptivity/relevance, or accomplishment, etc. The result of "static standard syndrome" is personal dissatisfaction, plus displaced/projected frustration within social networks that progressively (or regressively) curtail freedom in choosing alternate futures. Others should not use our identities as benchmarks to define *their* qualitative "selves."

b. Qualitative productivity is incorporated into a "Zero-Sum" relationship context, where "products" created or commodities "acquired" are theoretically, parallel transformed units of human "worth." As we gain these units, they are relinquished or "lost" by others (when I win, you lose).

c. Philosophic ideologies revolve around nonexistent levels of qualitative "domains" or "states" of being. This expenditure of attenuated energy could otherwise be saved, or used in enjoying the rewards of already "being" in a desired state. We spend considerable time becoming "that which one already was" (i.e., "I was perfect until I began believing that I was not perfect, then I had to work to acquire what I already had, and have now 'perceptually' lost").

d. Productivity evolves into a system of cultural "norms" for attitude and behavior. Rules produce physical "evidence" to (1) substantiate "differences" between people, (2) lead to assumptions of "free choice" of conforming or deviant behavior, (3) obscure patterns of political and economic "selectivity" of social opportunity, (4) obscure personal "non-choice" dimensions of culturally predestined "success" and "failure" (an upper-middle-class person can no more easily "achieve" poverty than a poor person can achieve "affluence"), (5) solidify beliefs and majority/minority activities that "trap" all groups in checkmated inertia patterns that waste resources, predispose "inferior" groups to costly "rehabilitations," or prevent improvement of material or "spiritual" life generally.

5. *"I'm Alone"*—The developmental *formula* in any child's mind may be a reflection of self-perceived independence and responsive freedom, relative to others who "share power" with them to meet needs reciprocally. It may also illustrate "energies," "essences," or processes of thinking or behaving that are entirely contained within the boundaries of each person's metabolic manifestation (cerebral electricity, thermoneurologic cell activity, affective stimulation, etc.). In both cases, excessive individualism evolves as an echo of *socially learned* "separateness," when "closeness" with parents was associated with conflictual "pain" (physical or emotional). The immutable "dependency indenture" of childhood implants a "human relationship" time capsule

in everyone's mind, regardless of its expressional width. Dependency ranges from (a) extensive closeness to demand more nurturance (symbiosis), to (b) "pseudo distance" to express *anger* (itself an associational insurance policy and inverted medium of connection) and alienation. Most of us balance the scales of reciprocal aloneness and togetherness somewhere between these diametric polarities, but accentuate one dimension of this continuum more than another. The "alone vs. together" controversy involves critical subdecisions, which combine to produce a personality "framework," to satisfy itself and facilitate emotional sustenance in others. This framework is opposed, necessarily, to the process of becoming frustrated, needy, and alienated from itself and others in its effort to achieve homeostatic "peace" within the living process. Components of associational perspective involve decisions concerning (a) whether reality exists *totally* as personal choice to perceive any set of concepts or objects; (b) whether human needs and feelings *require* input from other "feeling" creatures for fullest satisfaction; (c) determining if emotional relationships *actually* produce a "collective consciousness" which exists *beyond,* and as a synthesis of individual energies which interact; (d) deciding if relationship loss and pain therefrom is *normal,* rather than insufficient resolution of "self-other conflicts" by the "surviving party"; (e) the ability of the human organism to *ever* become fully one (complete efficiency, effectiveness, and pragmatic functionalism) with its primary nature, considering the mind's creation of dualistic symbols of itself (what Sartre calls the "for itself" rather than the "in itself"); and, (f) the possible existence of bio-metaphysical-spiritual-chemical-electrical "matrices" of interdependence among multiple "energy nuclei" (including human life force "centers") within the ecology.

One maladaptive danger of excessive belief in one's "aloneness" is a *formula* for explaining the nature of life. This is a hazard if the organism "naturally" requires human stimulation for optimum survival. Artificial isolation may result in use of excessive amounts of otherwise occupied energy, to create an artificial self-nurturing cybernetic system. This system, however, may never reach complete "fulfillment," or may distort reality to justify "quality" of life vis-a-vis the presumed necessity of suffering loneliness, to complete its solitary "destiny." If one chooses to be "victimized" by life process, there is always room for philosophic conjecture about whether "choice of pain" is really "pleasure."

Another concern for the "responsible" individual is whether any self-reinforcing formula for "autonomy" (aloneness) maintains functional boundaries which exclude stimulus-response relationships with other individuals. These might be people with whom we have "legitimized" psychosocial roles (parenting roles with our children), or individuals to develop facilitative "enabling" interactions. The possibility of one "original" set of parents for the entire human race suggests a naturalistic and evolutionary "world constellation" of brothers and sisters. We might share "familial lineage" and, therefore, possess a "bonded" bio-psychic unity and socio-heredity relative to everyone's welfare. Quite possibly, we may have become dissociated through fabrication of incorrect cause and effect mental concepts that exclude awareness and "sensation" of horizontal or vertical life forces that connect all people.

A less altruistic "rationale" for a non-idiosyncratic approach, involves systems theory's postulates of functional interdependence between all singular "units" of any organized apparatus. From a broad perspective, some "degree of aloneness" on our part stimulates a "response to aloneness" in some associated component of an inter-human world. This reaction may alter, to various extents, the overall product of the "collective consciousness." Most of us will neither believe, nor feel guilty about any *one* aspect of our "separation from others" which influences emotional distance. For example, we will not feel guilty about distance from our local mail carrier, who reciprocates with alienation toward someone he or she meets on vacation abroad, who, in turn, thinks or acts "responsively," which, through a chain of events, concludes with a terrorist somewhere in South America killing a Catholic sister. This chain affects our lives through a series of nearly imperceptible domino-like interactions throughout the world's complex veins and arteries of "every exchange." This may, however, be exactly how the "ball bounces."

There is another ramification of "believing" that the mind interacts predominantly with itself in some (a) conscious-to-unconscious, (b) foreground symbol-to-background symbol, or (c) introjected parent-to-child format. Psychic and bio-sensory energies may be diverted from alternative "planes" of awareness and "metabolization" which could render entirely different and revolutionary interpretations of all experiences and "not-yet experiences." The traumas of childhood survival may condition or predispose obsessions with securing the "necessities" of physical survival, which obfuscate maturation to "less desperate" sustenance ratios with the environment. Also, as power of cognition "explodes" in adolescence and adulthood, the mind unnecessarily precludes later-life attention to "higher realms" of existence.

This may extend even beyond artistic, religious, emotional and other culture-bound "meanings" experienced (often purchased) by those with inherited positions or predispositions to higher socioeconomic status. Although "searchers" seek interaction with "ultimate domains" of lifehood, "formulas" of entrenched self-centered concepts from early socialization, may imprison us in recapitulative "mental Xeroxing." We duplicate stimulus and response patterns that discourage open-ended exploration of awareness options. "Options" which are not familiar to us may be described by metaphysical or spiritual Masters, or experimenters with various forms of sensory manipulation (deprivation, drugs, mind control, electrical stimulation, psychotic thought processes), when they transcend the "normal" world of knowing and experiencing.

In a final example, medical and psychologic sciences have taught about psychophysiologic, psychosomatic, auto-hypnotic, and other self-induced or exacerbated "influences" on the body, which are generated by the mind. It is reasonable to conclude there may be direct "message conduits" between brain and other organ cells, in addition to the "indirect" influences we all recognize. These may manifest resultant physical (or associated mental) effects primarily because of the "directionality" (inward or intra-systemic) of the "energy vectors" which we pilot retroflectively toward ourselves. This preoccupation may, again, reflect "self-indulgent" conditioning from childhood, and cause suffering, medical maladies, or premature aging and death. Whether self-stimulated physiologic deterioration is "responsible" or not, it certainly seems contradictory to the commonly accepted "spirit or quest for life" in all cultures.

6. *"I'm Together"*—Long childhood dependency, plus "socially" conscious culture, instills a range of orientations concerning our linkages to other people, both proximate and distant in genealogy. Time, energy, money, conceptual speculation, grief and mourning, and other reactions revolve around the formulation, maintenance, dissolution, re-creation, veneration and recollection of interpersonal configurations of "togetherness." Most cultures, of course, have defined rituals for handling "togetherness" concerns, and view relationship decisions and emotions as a relatively personal realm of vivification. It is still necessary to reflect, however, on the basic *nature* and *value* of traditional concepts of interpersonal relations. Some philosophic questions are these:

   a. To what extent does "unity" with someone else represent an artificial overlap or amalgamation of "energies"? Does connection magnetically bind attention, and focus it away from personal "needs" which must be fulfilled individually?

b. Does participation in "programmed interchange" limit behavioral/attitudinal options for fuller self-expression? Does it "condition" states of "being" which are dictated by shared "evaluative power," rather than personal intentions to "be" as one chooses?

c. Are varying degrees of closeness related to greater satisfactions of adult needs versus regressions to childhood dependencies? How do any of us more comprehensively pursue "depth" in "shared perceptions"?

d. Is the interconnected domain of "we-ness" a separate condition of phenomenologic reality, a re-creation of parent-child relational "states," or perceptions by each individual which are achievable, given modifications of ideology, through exclusive intrapsychic process?

e. What is the *range* of "relevant" relationship interest and potential, and does energy investment in near vs. distant "connections," influence any outcomes of individual behavior (e.g., altered voting choices resulting from perception of relationship with a Russian person[s])?

f. What capabilities are necessary to utilize psychic or physical "vibrations" from another person? What is the "ratio" of individual-to-joint sensory and cognitive awareness to discover and benefit from the life-force of someone else (do I give up "we-ness" beliefs before I direct "individual" energy to accomplish a more qualitative interpersonal conjunction)?

7. *"I Am or I Am Not"*—This final section of problematic frameworks, which minds utilize to explain "reality" (or lack thereof) and guide behaviors, is more esoteric than the previous six categories of "am-ness." It represents principles applied to each previous category, but accompanying "interstitial" postulates which may improve the "quality" of our lives, or lives of those who *depend on us* to define the "self." Most agree that (a) we "exist," (b) we perceive physical objects pretty much in congruence with their *actual* natures, (c) there was some "First Cause" of life in the universe, and (d) there are principles of living which routinely work better than others as social "truths." There may, however, be finer sub-dimensions of (a) perceptions of "relativity" of

being, (b) subjective irrationality (or failure to discover rationality, unrationality or not-rationality), or (c) creative symbolic pretense, which constitutes the critical "qualitative aspect" of human ontology and axiology (being and value). Differentiations of "existence" perspectives may help each reader understand the degree to which there are particular "valences" of hierarchical *pertinence, permanence* or *knowability* (epistemology) of life. These conditions of being, influence the responsibilities we undertake in relationships between "selves" and other "phenomena," with which we negotiate and insure survival. The following "qualifiers," therefore, allow emphasis of alternate validity-confirming or denying beliefs, and guide the assignment of value indices (and converse need-deprivations) to life concepts. They help us evaluate the "worth" of our lives—as we utilize various "worth" viewpoints to categorize thoughts and events:

a. *Humor* directed at humanity *suggests* we are not as "significant" as we would like to believe. We *may enhance* life through tension reduction, reframing behavioral options, or reducing the impact of arbitrary values applied to specific situations.

b. Mitigation of expended *efforts* (don't try so hard) may redirect attention from "outcome" to "process," or from "becoming" to "being." It may enhance enjoyment, by emphasizing the arbitrary and situationally irrelevant aspects of particular goals.

c. Relaxation of *ultra-sensitivity* to the "self" (I am "not" to the degree I could "be") may reduce guilt and other self-indulgent "entrapments." These occur within narrowly conceived and conflictual paradigms of relationships (past or present) or intra-cognitive "debates."

d. Emphasis on a *valued "self"* for its "own sake" may guide us away from destructive actions of others. It may also reinforce "healthy" relationships, thoughts, feelings and activities which have more extensive and intensive "positive" orientations of life.

e. Diminishing perspectives of the relevance of any condition of "being," may reduce prejudicial judgments which limit opportunities of others to "be more fully." Discriminations arise because we are afraid of the insignificance of not being ourselves, and defensively exaggerate the "am-ness" of the self, or denigrate this phenomenon in someone else.

Conclusion

In concluding this chapter on "growing" psychosocially, and understanding pitfalls in interpreting mental formulae which represent developmental outcomes, I should like to present a list of "qualitative" guides for thinking about the self. These ideas reduce conflict and psychic distress, create self-acceptance and unity of identity, and improve the quality and functionality of relationships.

Guidelines for viewing developmental processes and outcomes are as follows:

1. Remember the person we "are," in actuality, may have no other substances than electrical brain waves or "sparks," and cellular physiology (chemical blood, bone material, organ tissue, etc.). This view suggests careful analysis of "feelings," "values," and "selves" to which we attribute a "corporeal identity." This identity becomes a "solid phenomenon" in our minds, which (a) can be "hurt" emotionally, (b) can "fail" or be "rejected," (c) becomes angry and retaliatory toward others, and (d) can actually *kill* members of the same species in the name of "virtue or honor." How does "honor," for example, become animated within the context of electricity, which constitutes its (honor's) existence only symbolically?

2. Goals and objectives we pursue, together with foundation "values" which punctuate their "relevance," may exist only as symbolic extensions of physical developmental traumas, crises and survival needs. Despite cultural validation of "higher order" needs and destinies, the preponderance of effort to "become" something of a "superior nature," may be nothing more than transformed animalistic instincts to stay alive. This conjectural awareness might lessen anxiety, frustration, confusion and even physical tedium which accompanies struggles and disappointments to scale a possible irrelevant hierarchy of "esoteric statuses." We may benefit from re-examination of the pressure for competitive achievement for adults and children when, in "fact" we may exert too much effort "getting all dressed up, with no place to go."

3. We might consider the importance played by childhood fear and dependency, which become vividly ingrained on impressionable young memories. They possibly remain as critical influences on life decisions, from the highly impregnable "command post" of the mind's unconscious. In this light, socially supported values, aspirations, and achievements may represent "regressive" defenses against "real-but-outdated" or "irrational" trepidations, rather than "progressive" accomplishments of "ethereal woman/man." Self-righteousness and truth-possessing isolation that accompanies

ethnocentrism, plus support for personal or family virtue, may pinpoint weakness rather than strength. *Vulnerability* may be a common thread uniting us to one another, which further suggests "sameness" rather than "discriminative variation" is the salvation of intercultural and inter-human relationships.

4. "Closeness" or "distance" within expectations and communicational operations of relationships, may represent recapitulative "formulae" or blueprints developed and socialized throughout childhood. They may reflect needs and reality perceptions of "then-superior/controlling" authority figures, rather than functional needs of our adult selves. Compliance to "estranged" models of "oneness-with-self" or "togetherness-with-other" may result in counterproductive pursuits of an illusion of "perfected conformity" to prescripted guidelines. These pursuits may, conveniently, prevent more fulfilling animations of psychic and physical energy in an alternate scenario. Examples of entrapment in previously engineered, but subjective axiomatic "opinions" about life, include (a) the single person's pursuit of a "normal heterosexual relationship," (b) "laws" concerning the need for children to please parents, (c) concepts of "oneness" in marriage, (d) beliefs in personal "autonomy and independence," and (e) public prescriptions of "socially conforming behavior" as a value in and of itself.

5. Beliefs about the "nature" of person and "destiny" of humanity may be highly correlated with contemporary historical technology, organizational configurations, resource availabilities, and subsistence practices (getting food, controlling body temperature, etc.). These demographics, however, may become "controlling monsters" we create to insure *our* survival. They may exploit their own systems, through the media and various marketing philosophies, to maintain *their own* survival, and the illusion of sanity and security in a confusing world. We are taught that "we are," relative to "what needs to be done" to survive physically. Gaps or changes in the evolution of technology and economy as they consume and destroy their own raw materials before creating new ones (e.g., wood-coal-oil-nuclear power); are also explained as "normal." Complex, capitalistic society has tragic consequences on its human "victims" (the poor, consumers, working classes, minorities) which are justified by *associated* religious, spiritual or philosophic overarching models of transcendent reality.

We may benefit by remembering that the "meaning of life" has changed substantially with each major period of history. We may (a) "know" only what we "do," (b) think "right" is only what "works now," (c) believe "who" we are is "who *we* tell ourselves we are," and (d) depend on spiritual or religious explanations of "greater" meaning, value and relevance. Spirituality, however, is often ignored when physical survival is believed to be at stake (we justify killing the same species, despite the fact that religions and humanistic philosophies insist that people should not destroy other people). Religion also serves as ideologic "mortar" to fill the gaps in human need, to discover relevance beyond mere animalistic sustenance of physical life.

Chapter II

POVERTY, CRIME, AND DRUG ABUSE

The above social ills represent stages of life's drama upon which are enacted horrible "scripts" of suffering, privation, alienation, fear, anger, hatred, and self/social destruction. "Advantaged" citizens view these phenomena as relatively "peripheral" (although theoretically important) dimensions of their lives, or as isolated "exposures," or *crises* in otherwise successful and healthy existence. I intend no criticism, that most of us avoid social "negatives," and prefer "achievement" to grow beyond the self-curtailment of economic insufficiency, gross social deviance, chemical dependency, etc. Negative "images" of the conditions and personages which characterize this "nether-world" are most comfortably obscured for us all, including the direct participants in the "garbage cans" of life. Knowledge of this world is hidden within the psyche's unconscious "black box," or concealed behind "lily-white" catechisms, doctrines, or faiths which "justify" "self-destruction" through various overarching principles. Typical distancing *philosophies* to "sweeten the air" are these: self-determination, predestination, justice, deferred gratification, reincarnation, holism, spiritual exaltation of sufferers, rewards of productivity, genetic inferiority/superiority, natural selection, religious preparation for rebirth, Karmic debt and learning, self-delusion, eco-cosmic synergization, ecclesiastical retribution, purgatorial transition, ancestral and spirit pontification, or existential irrelevance, etc., etc., etc.

In any case, *negative social circumstances* and associated psychophysical pain *exist,* whether relevant to correlated purposes, origins, or distant horizons of the universe at large. There is a difficult challenge, obviously, in relating variable "exogenous" life situations of sufferers within sociocultural categories, to "endogenous" mainstream awarenesses and "relevancies." Our life concerns are usually far removed from "real" issues of economic failure and starvation, heroine/cocaine addiction, penal imprisonment, problem-solving with fists/knives/guns, theft/personal assault/murder/sexual perversion, etc., etc., or daily struggles with despair/depression/role loss/inferior health/fear-anxiety/discrimination, or social injustice. To integrate diametric polarities of "successful social adaptation," requires several hypotheses which suggest the import of this topic on every person who lives on the earth.

Hypotheses Concerning Social Adaptation

Social "dysfunctions" of *large,* homogeneous *groups* (the poor, criminal subcultures, drug abuse networks, etc.) reflect *system-wide* and generalized *profiles* of communities. Their "normal" patterns of work, resource allocation, transaction of monetary exchange, benefit disbursement, property ownership, domestic residence, travel proclivities, and philosophic values; actually *authorize* and *produce benefit* from the negative experiences and "choice enclaves" available to disenfranchised groups. Although many disagree with this societal "balance" framework, its systems theory principles insist that phenomena do not maintain continuity unless there are rewards *everywhere* within a network of "interactive units of energy." We all "participate," therefore, in maintaining counterbalancing forces of poverty, crime, etc. by directly or intermittently receiving material or psychologic *benefits* of the following:

1. "Aversive documentation" is something we need to "see" occasionally, or "sense" emotionally. Negatives (a) substantiate the rationale for, and encourage investment in *mainstream approaches* to life ("Work hard, Junior, so you don't end up like those poor people"). Negative circumstances also insure that (b) what we do for entire lifetimes can be judged relevant (thesis vs. antithesis), so that (c) the "pain" of human life is "justified."

2. Economic (lower-class) consumer markets for mainstream industrial "waste products" or inexpensive commodities, are necessary for social life as it is now organized. These products are produced rapidly at little cost, with minimal quality control and low retail overhead. They stimulate cash flow to support more costly, "slower moving," but higher-profit "primary" products. These markets provide management and staff jobs for "working" and middle-class society, and curtail *losses* on production by-products (e.g., cheap toys for poor kids can be made from waste rubber, metals, etc.; inexpensive clothing can be produced with cheap "foreign" labor). Quality control standards maintained for middle and upper-class society are sidestepped, to avoid consumer litigation for inferior materials/workmanship. Inferior goods are purchased quickly by "deprived consumers" who thus have *some* of the benefits of life.

3. We think we need a "cheap" supply of menial labor, where minimal employment benefits and wages enhance profit margins "at the top" of organizations and businesses. These insure basic "maintenance" functions because of (a) extreme competition for jobs, (b) absence of influential "demands" for employee benefits, (c) easy compliance with affirmative action government standards, and (d) performance and attitude manipulation because of inferior self-esteem, dependency, and fear of job loss.

4. Ready sources of cost-effective personal services (servants) for mainstream society (a) are utilized on intermittent, employer-demand schedules, (b) can be "rented" without employee benefits or prohibitive income tax constrictions, and (c) come without expectations of personal relationships or "deferential treatment" from employers. "Po folks" can be utilized for difficult or unpleasant tasks with minimal aversion or refusal to comply with employer demands (e.g., yard services, ironing and washing clothes, babysitting, prostitution, etc.).

5. The world needs "denials" through (a) social outlet for anger at our own projected "badness," (b) tension release through punishment of lawbreakers, and (c) validation (inversely and comparatively) of mainstream "sanctity" (real or imaginary). We also take advantage of opportunities for (d) rationalization of less destructive and comparatively minor "white-collar" crimes, through comparison of gross pathologies to "socially responsible behavior." Finally, the "haves" (e) vicariously enjoy guilt-free impulsive hedonism as symbolized by dramatic personalities of cultural outlaws, who are *admired* and *destroyed* by an observing audience. We do not "pay the price" of direct confrontation between opposing inner psychic drives, needs, and forces.

6. Lucrative markets for "illegitimate and illegal" products (especially drugs) and controlled substances (legitimate drugs and alcohol) provide several benefits: (a) a predictable "constituency" of *dependent* consumers who pay exorbitant prices, which (b) supports an underground "black market" world economy that provides employment for working class men and women, but also (c) provides "duty-free" capital to underwrite legal business ventures supported through syndicated organized crime organizations, plus (d) provides substantial secondary legitimate revenue to mainstream corporate enterprise.

7. We benefit from receptive "contingents" of "needy clientele" for various spiritual/emotional/psychological *service delivery functions* intending to improve "quality of life." Victims constitute an appreciative outlet for (a) charitable acts and donations which provide gratification to "humane"

intents of "fortunate" citizens, and allow a (b) fertile arena for "social change" efforts, and inexpensive fulfillment of norms for emotional caring. These "outcomes" have an illusionary high *effectiveness quotient* when baseline deprivation levels of "have nots" can be substantially augmented (or failure rationalized) with minimal expenditures from the affluent "haves." However, deprived populations remain an insignificant challenge due to their own subcultural obstacles which "hold them in place."

This benefit is especially true as a monetary and organizational support structure for human service workers, whose psycho-philosophic ideologies render them unproductive in other areas of the work force. Governmental agencies employ massive "non-professional" support staffs, in relatively permanent job positions. These roles balance the "ups and downs" of frontline industrial productivity, sustain middle-class consumer groups in their leisure and recreational pursuits, and provide a "social control" function to manage deviation. There is, herein, provision for a "politically defensible" justification for tax increases—the belief that social compliance is enhanced when large dollar amounts (but small percentages) are used humanely. This mirage diverts attention from substantive tax profits invested in goods, services, and remunerations for more affluent groups.

Collectively, "successful" members of the middle and upper classes derive substantive *benefit* (through indirect contributions of labor, cash flow, or ideologic status) from economic and governmental "benevolencies"; these benefits provide the hidden supports of the system. This transaction occurs, unfortunately, via the plight of "deviants," within noncompetitive economic and work strata, who survive as "symbolic referents" for philosophies of mainstream society. They strive to "become" successful through the much needed expenditure (not saving) of "cash" dollars and the predictability of their consumer profiles for inexpensive industrial "by-products." Understanding the "natures" of these socially "deviant, needy and deprived" groups, helps us understand the meaning of our own status, and encourages appreciation of the full *range* of psychosocial *phenomena* which exist in the world.

Parallel Adaptational Formulas in Different Cultures

There is a second reason poverty and associated crime and drug abuse are significant to the community at large (parallel "white-collar" illegalities and "high society" drug abuse/alcoholism also exist). Dynamic psychological and social "energies," decision-making patterns, and collective behavioral "forces" which create and maintain "cultures" of poverty—are *identical* to the formulas for adaptation of *all other* "social-strata" groups and "ideo-thetic" collectivities in the world. Knowing this, per se, does not lead to engagement with the "ethos" of the poverty phenomenon. What does, however, *involve everyone* in ecologic-universalism of the "thetic and antithetic" balance of life, is *realization* that non-poverty classes are *equally trapped* in tightly-woven interdependencies. Cognitive/emotional needs for autonomous relevance are on one side of the equation, with culture-confirming security structures on the other. Although there is some satisfaction in reaping the benefits ("victor-conqueror or victor-victim") within either hemisphere, the "whole" self remains "impoverished" in this process. *Energies* to rationalize *either* dimension of survival, and "conditioned perspectives" to maintain membership in only a portion of life's scenario—are supported by "oppositional domains" balancing all phases of existence and process (light/dark, summer/winter, birth/death, male/female, etc.). From a "physical comforts" viewpoint, any "sane" person who is not poor would loathe "submersion" into this morass of suffering and disappointment. But, inhabitants of poverty subcultures *also experience* dissonant adjustment and transitional blockages in those few cases where economic advantages become available. Unfortunately for them, "old" ways of believing and feeling must surrender to traditional higher socioeconomic "class" categories and cultural frameworks.

(1) If the "haves" maintain current success and status through fears of becoming "have nots," and (2) if "have nots" are viewed with denotative or connotative negativism (relative to intelligence, ambition, lifestyle, etc.) by those who "seem" more prosperous; then (3) the *full* definition of a prosperous "self" demands an "inverted" corresponding image of "loss or privation." This maintains a clearer "resolution" of the "gain or attribution" image of identity. Successes that depend upon moving *away* from a negative condition may represent "regression" to an aversive-dependent relationship with a form of being we deny ("not" or "negative" being). Herein, perceptions of current success are obscured or remain invisible. "Success" only has relevance when "non-success" forms the reflective backdrop which creates the meaning of *not* non-success, which we call success. This argument holds for people who cling to limited life "pleasures" because they fear tragedy of "non-pleasure" during the absence of life (not "death" necessarily, but "non-life"). Absence of pleasure/pain tension suggests that pain does not exist beyond the existential realm of life, so pleasure is not pleasure at all, but non-pain. To some, not having pain, or having non-life, may be equal, or superior to having life, with pain that interfaces with pleasure. "Nonexistence" in "current" life forms, therefore, may not be validly compared to "nonexistence" in unknown constitutions of the self/non-self domain. The rationale for valuation of what "is" (that which we know) only makes "sense" when compared to another dimension of what "also is." This is contradistinctive to a definition of what "is not" (and has "not yet been," or "never was" known to the living mind—vs. the non-living mind which may only function when we are not living).

In this balancing of life process, the "haves" maintain an unconscious vested interest in the continuation of poverty. This "vests" us to support the ideological value of "having what we have," but also represents an *aversive condition* which provides "productivity energy" to justify that life is valuable. We envision concrete examples of "negative" or "non-valuable" life, to dispel lingering childhood fears of the *existential unknown,* which we choose to name "non-life," "non-thought," "non-feeling," etc. Those in poverty are caught in a similar "existential" trap, although obvious benefits of physical comfort validate the "relevance" of mainstream life. The poor person has a greater reason for *being,* in one perspective, because the materialistic ladder has a large number of rungs "up ahead." The "rich" however, ultimately run out of material satisfactions, and revert to ideologic and spiritual rationales for the validity of life.

In understanding structural poverty, it is important to realize that "poor" conditions of life emanated anthropologically as a by-product of "instinctual" animalistic superiority and territorial control. Animals (human prototypes) were "accidentally" born with richer eco-environmental habitants and species attributional characteristics, and evolved to become better nourished, stronger, and more capable of dominating physical space. The "survivors" used "inferior" species for physical sustenance and secondary by-products (animal skins for covering, bones for tools, etc.). In-breeding naturally produced continuations of "ruling classes" (genus and species) and parallel extensions of complementary prey organisms. Both groups were genetically and socially programmed to understand their respective life destinies. They developed extrapolative behavioral capabilities and evolving physical characteristics to survive and proliferate the species. In some cases, maturational advantage may have been boosted by ecological protections, nutritional sufficiencies, survival demands of the environment (or lack thereof for other species), or "chance" occurrences.

As homo sapiens emerged, incredible "reasoning" capabilities "selected" women and men as superior "sovereignties." Our species is apparently "plagued" however by three inherent deficits: (1) continuous retro-primordial "instinct" for survival, including endogenous fear of extinction and aversion to physical pain and starvation; (2) still-limited mental abilities for omniscient understanding of ultimate truth, and inability to obliterate apprehension, internal conflict, confusion, self-absorption; and finally (3) inevitable mortality. In non-Darwinian, and "creationist," belief systems about the origin and sacrosanct or acquisitional journey of human life (soul, spirit, self, etc.), the above limitations materialize with these "asterisked" notations:

1. Personkind "earned" mortal life-form and circumstance through "chosen alienation" from a benevolent God or "Super-Force" ("man" ate fruit of the

tree of knowledge of good and evil [ambivalence and conflict] and, through disloyalty and mistrust, suffers with "knowledge" until re-earning "Grace").

2. The struggle for survival was not inherited directly, but "rendered" as punishment; or a motivational process illustrates negative consequences of free-will and selfishness.

3. Loss of "knowing" universal truth was not a natural biologic inheritance, but a "relegational burden" that followed illusions of power.

4. The search for "God" is accompanied by stringent requirements of faith and dedicated "service," which result from "profane" negligence of inaugurative spiritual and physical "gifts."

As culture encapsulated and accentuated "essences" of evolutionary or created "humanoidism," conditions of *vulnerable mortality* persisted. Our status was "achieved" ecologically with remaining limitations, or inherited from a superordinate "power," with deficits to be overcome with final rewards. These requirements or necessities received progressively "symbolic" expression within agricultural, industrial, community service and economic systems. They included (1) creating "production" for survival, (2) regulating consumer acquisition of "equilibrated" goods and services, (3) insuring product and energy "profits" to overcome ecologic obstacles when natural supply is exhausted, (4) controlling deviations from orderly exchange of needs and benefits, (5) creating monetary systems for an expanding populace, and (6) developing ideology to "fill in the gaps" while waiting for natural death. Overarching societal "processes" continue to maintain "king of the jungle" mentalities. Competitive frameworks are upheld through institutionalization of expectations for individual (and family) achievement and through maintenance of capitalistic business (production and sales) networks. The "pulse of life" is measured by standards of aggressiveness, initiatory surprise, win/lose criteria, control of vulnerable consumer markets, and defeat of competitive enterprises. All these systems show linear attachment to the basic "survival format" of both current and primordial animal species. Although culture developed humanitarian and social "functions" to enhance dignity and opportunity of people everywhere, the survival, even of these benevolent activities, is predicated on shrewd manipulations and contra-distinctive philosophies. These occur in political arenas of funding and decisioning, relative to "constituent" priorities, needs, and remunerations.

Current mechanisms of competitive advantage and aptitude, furthermore, are undergirded by socialized views of the "self" and the world which reflect early childhood "training." Successful (adaptive) parents produce mirrored offspring who are "computer programmed" to perceive a "lucrative" generalized *destiny;*

and "have nots" teach only the negatives they "know" and have experienced. Successive generations of disenfranchised citizens (1) expect to be "victims of superior gladiators," and (2) spend "learning" time figuring out, from role models and observations of poverty, what attitudes and behaviors are mandatory to survive emotionally and validate the self spiritually, within the *realistic* "opportunities" available. In cases of rich, poor and in-betweens, subsistence is the "bottom line," followed by "spiritual ventures" among all social stratifications, to prove the relevancy of existence. "Higher" realms of self-actualization, however, are symbolized differently for each social group, and are "paid for" with some similar, but many different, types of exchange "tender." Everyone "purchases" aspirational and inspirational heaven on/after earth in some way, as long as no one has demonstrated transcendence beyond the limitations of human thought, fear, anxiety, loneliness, pain, or death. Every vulnerable human mind (psyche, soul, spirit, emotion, etc.) is identical in basic biology and mechanical function, although symbolic icons and "adaptational" referents are different for the dominating vs. dominated animal classes. For those trapped in a culture of poverty inherited from ancestral "victims" of a "fitter" predator species, there is an indelible set of learned principles, values of surviving, and behavioral patterns which are "concretized" within childhood memory banks. They result from parental and peer teaching, experiential modeling, and *negative injunction* from mainstream individuals and institutions which reject outsiders. The reverse occurs with learning in the "dominant success" culture, although fewer attempts at infiltration are experienced by minority or poor subcommunities, and culture does not advertise the ideals of "lower" socioeconomic status as admirable life goals. Principles of learned stratification, alienation, and victimization of the "under classes" are as follows:

1. "Every generation of your relatives has desired greater success and *failed.* The probability that you will contradict this pattern is extremely unlikely."

2. "Success images you observe and are 'presented' with in all forms of media require education, money, personal connections, physical health, and supportive environments which are permanently unavailable to you."

3. "Affluence requires substantial deferred gratification, which is followed by expanded social opportunities. These are closed to you because of (a) 'who' you are culturally, (b) your lack of skill-building—denied by untrained parents, (c) the shortness of time you have for gratuitous preparation because of 'survival' necessities, and (d) recurrent interruptions in your growing environment. You demonstrate [1] disjunctive and minimal efforts to succeed in an economic environment that will reject you, and [2] social and psychological 'randomness' of 'success-oriented' thoughts, emotions and behaviors, caused by frustration and despair."

4. "There is little value in postponing physical and emotional pleasure while awaiting 'higher' material and social goals that will be systematically denied to you. Immediate gratification of impulses is the only rational approach to a life of prolonged deprivation and discrimination."

5. "Believing that 'successful society' cares about you is insane, and rarely dispelled by efforts on 'their' part to improve 'your gain.' You will feel frustrated anger at 'losing to winners' who control your destiny."

6. "Efforts to integrate mainstream values or lifestyles alienates you from your own 'roots,' and causes rejection from the self-serving upper class. It insures discomfort in changing major perspectives of truth and reality—therefore it is easiest and most comfortable to conform to *your* status quo."

From the standpoint of broad-based economic and political systems, competitive and "survivalistic" capitalism "advances" by populating its productive work force with its most qualified, skilled, innovative, energetic, conforming, and aspiring employees. Society supports conservative and "stable" consumer markets by providing the greatest advantage to advocates of capitalistic productivity. Those supporters, in turn, purchase large quantities of their own products to compensate for higher salaries, and develop "advanced" symbolic systems of "complex" conceptualizaton and feeling as part of their systemic roles. This creates a vast market for leisure-time "cultural" goods and services which controls impulse (which leads to deviance if unchanneled), and stimulates expansion of esoteric realms of human validity. "Advanced" cultural benefits can be purchased at profit-bearing costs, and "spiritual" and "emotional" norms categorically control and manipulate the "masses."

The poor, of course, cannot get richer in this zero-sum system, nor is there advantage in elevating their employment capabilities because (1) "menial" work remains a necessity, and (2) "animalistic predatory" theories and methods of alienational production (competitors and natural resources are obstacles to be conquered) produce fewer jobs in mainstream industry. In the long run, increased job competition would benefit entrepreneurial management with lower wage demands and increased profits. Unfortunately, sufficiently high-middle, and upper-middle-class birthrates, and prohibitive "rehabilitative" costs for the poor, mitigate against plans for "balancing the scales." Because middle classes defer "pleasure-principaled gratification" to obtain "higher-order" esoteric or materialistic goals, they (we) respond to intermittent reinforcement systems (like slot machines in Las Vegas). Government and industry do not have to expend profit resources all at once, to stimulate society's continued use of productive energy. Therefore, continued labor is insured, plus periodic increases in creative and energetic investments can be predicted (based on reward potentials) when industry changes direction to adapt to voracious "outrunning" of its potential, and routine exhaustion of raw materials.

The poor are hired with minimal profit-depleting wages or fringe benefits, yet constant stimulation of cravings causes perceptions of deprivation and "salivation" at the marketplace. This insures cash expenditures for predictably needed goods and services. The poor are socialized with an alienational "mind-set" relative to middle-class fear of, and lack of interest in them. As a consequence, disenfranchised groups develop cultural patterns and values which necessarily differentiate themselves from their predators (government officials, property owners, social control agents, production managers, pecuniary lenders, etc.). The alienated (1) do not experience devastating "cognitive dissonance" by *believing* they are like the "haves," but "do not have what the haves have," (2) they develop emotional defensive explanations of why they are too cold, too hot, too hungry, too "stupid," etc., with burdens of responsibility on "social victimization" which is not their fault, or on alternative personal value preferences they can control, and (3) they develop *ideologic* beliefs which place reward contingencies outside the material control functions of majority society, seen as more powerful in terms of money, land, food, police, media. These value systems include massive doses of fundamental and evangelical religion. Finally, (4) the disenfranchized "romanticize" *outlaw* mentalities which controls guilt and justifies overt or covert expressions of resistance and offensive attack on those who control independent choice and opportunity.

Although some poverty dwellers accomplish "crossover" upward mobility, most *do not* because of the following:

1. They are fundamentally "taught" that life, for them, is a process of *losing,* wherein they accept a *victim role,* enjoy immediate pleasures, and lower their *own* aspirations to minimize disappointment.

2. They live for "today only," since accumulated capital is never sufficient to purchase stability or an inspired future (property, education, health care, entertainment).

3. Recurrent job and personal/family instability caused by market fluctuations (marginal workers are expendable when profits diminish), chronic deteriorative health, depression-based irresponsibility and impulsiveness, and inability to plan "rationally" within an uncertain environment—contribute to "peripheral" social roles.

4. Their social network sees no benefit in competing for status and positions which are withheld or unavailable. Therefore, "learning preparations" receive negative reinforcement to the point of virtual extinction.

5. Chronic low income produces susceptibility to random fates, disasters, or losses, where poor people never "get their heads above water" and eventually stop trying.

6. Daily survival in a drug, crime and suffering-filled world necessitates "maladaptive" (adaptive for them) personality traits which generate "hysterical excitement" to enjoy the drama of violent and highly "variable" slum life. "Sociopathic hardness" insulates them from emotional pain, supports a manipulative approach to satisfy survival needs, and justifies "paranoid-like distrust" to help them prepare for disappointing setbacks and upper-class rejections.

It is important to remember, of course, that those privileged to enjoy benevolent material circumstances, have also been taught to disdain the status, values, behaviors and general ethos of the "poor life." We are equally *incapable* of embracing and succeeding in "their" world. We are also simultaneously bound to the ideologies of mainstream "truth" which we can neither invalidate nor relinquish without disruption of beliefs which justify "where we are" as the "correct place to be."

Crime, Drug Abuse and Poverty

Crime, of course, exists at all levels of stratified life, but flourishes in its most violent and seemingly random forms within "lower-class" environments. Specifics of "acted out" alienation through crime are as follows:

1. Many suffering people are chronically *angry* and disappointed, and "animal natures" instinctively produce aggression to resolve crises of fear, and overcome insurmountable odds to meet basic needs.

2. Self-perceived and socially perpetuated "victim roles" allow easy justification for "irreverent" disruptions of mainstream social patterns. Caste systems create "scapegoat identities" for social groups, where power is obtained by causing crime-related pain and inconvenience.

3. Criminal activity receives minimal scrutiny in poverty neighborhoods, and therefore has a higher success rate. Also, "delinquency" enjoys *vicarious*

social support as an idealistic "outlaw" mentality which is the only power available in disenfranchised lives.

4. Unemployment means time available for criminal lifestyles, while upper-class victims are preoccupied with other concerns, making an inviting target of retaliation ("tally-again").

5. Crime provides quick and lucrative (although temporary) "solutions" to chronic need-deprivation problems, and produces immediate despair-fighting gratification.

6. Unconscious guilt over "failure" is dramatically enacted through official "social punishment." This forces a withholding society to take care of its floundering children (food in jail, shelter, clothing, *attention*), but makes the symbolized guilt palatable. The victim is justified in fighting "oppression," which is further validated when punishment ensues at the hands of upper-class controlled police, courts, penal systems, etc.

7. Violent acts and impulsive outbreaks provide (a) immediate psychodynamic reductions of lifelong frustrations, (b) perceived "solutions" to problems which require conceptualization and interpersonal skills poorly developed in underclass "mentality," (c) dramatic excitation in sterile or debilitating emotional milieus, and (d) expressions of power through physical or mechanical force (knives, guns, etc.).

Drug abuse *thrives* in poverty situations also, because of endogenous characteristics of this total life environment:

1. Drugs (and alcohol) provide anesthetic "numbing" sensations, and "transcendent" elevational functions. This occurs through "speeding" physio-neurologic process, creating mind altering hallucinatory "journeys," or inhibiting ego defenses. Independent impulses and emotions are expressed as desperate "escape mechanisms" relative to disparaging destinies of poverty subcultures.

2. The illegal status of "uncontrolled substances" necessitates their manufacture, storage, marketing and distribution within disorganized, non-litigational, distracted and "socially ignored" neighborhoods. Herein, detection and prosecution (except limited and highly publicized "sacrificial lamb" cases) are less probable.

3. Perpetration of destructive and frequently fatal drug utilization requires guilty and sublimational/projective "angry" victims among representatives,

at all levels, of the "drug business." This requires the antecedent "breeding ground" of large numbers of alienated, sociopathic, deviant, poverty-produced personnel (a smaller proportion of high-level leaders emerge as drug dealers, managers, etc.).

4. The drug business requires an untraceable and easily manipulable/ transferable cash economy wherein "impulse buying" produces immediate profits to pay subsidiary "employees." Moderate amounts of easy access funding must be available to consumers, especially via rapid acquisition methods of robbery, burglary, gambling and "protection rackets," etc.

5. Drugs and alcohol symbolize *dependency*, which allows people in unstable, arbitrary, and negativistic environments to exercise "some" control over their perceptions, moods, and feelings. At the same time, they do not have to assume responsibility, since independence will "situationally" result in "failure." Also, the destructive effects of abuse parallel depressive psychodynamics, where the personality punishes itself unconsciously for childhood and public recriminations of "its" inadequacies. These weaknesses and disabilities are blatantly measured in industrial societies by materialistic achievement standards.

Social Impacts of Drugs and Crime

Given personal "losses" in poverty, drug abuse, and crime—offset by some socioeconomic and political gains—my "punch line," illustrates the *impact of these social maladies* on those of us who are not directly affected. Society-wide and upper-class "negative outcomes" may require history's "parade" for a long time before "empirical" destructive results for universal humanity are realized. In some cases, the reader will only "perceive" *effects* on themselves and generations of their children, if they subscribe to certain metaphysical or spiritual philosophies which represent atypical (for mainstream society) "variables" and relationship "formulas" for holistic dynamics of life. In other cases, impacts are easily translatable or directly observed with quantitative and deductive reasoning, concerning gains or losses of commodities or symbolic exchange tokens. In all cases, however, I hope that all of you examine for yourselves the implications of simultaneous interaction of poverty and affluence within the same world "community."

1. *Money:* The easiest "loss" for affluent society to validate is economic. In these cases, (a) extraordinary amounts of funding are diverted from salaries or employment benefits of mainstream workers, or from public works, education, cultural activities, social security, health care, etc. These funds

are (b) plunged into massive social welfare programs. In most cases, "safety net" efforts (1) only "maintain" substandard levels of existence, (2) infrequently apply to *solutions* of problems, (3) support enormous institutional frameworks of bureaucracy whose potential is always underutilized, and (4) support perpetual dependency among noncontributing and unproductive masses of humanity. Other than maintaining minimal, but still deplorable levels of existence, this money is *wasted* on its targets, and denied to other projects of community life.

Also, there are long-term losses of commercial productivity and innovative resource development when *billions* of dollars are diverted to "correct" self-depreciation, despondency, anger, and irresponsibility. There is loss for everyone whose lives depend on: discoveries of new energy and food sources, development of workable relationships between alienated international societies, research into controls and elimination of physical and mental disease and uncomfortable metabolic aging, and management of living arrangements and property for growing numbers of community residents.

2. *Community Destruction:* Slum living conditions represent massive deterioration of land, fiscal property, and ecological atmosphere, including expansion of "spillover contamination" into other neighborhoods. Poverty populations "incubate" and export justifiably unappreciative and resentful attitudes and behaviors to other areas of the environment. In modern societies, middle-class populations generally ignore and circumvent low income housing neighborhoods, although effort and time are certainly expended in this "avoidance" process. Periodic exposure to this "aversive aesthetic stimulus" must, at some level of need for sensate pleasure, cost each of us mental or affective "dissonance," whereas neuro-perceptual energies might otherwise be utilized more productively. Every culture "needs itself" to validate its relevance. To this extent, poverty populations regenerate, as adults need love and creative opportunity to produce children, and as the group itself provides "insulation" against fear and extinction by procreative multiplication. Having children is one recreational and "life-force" opportunity that cannot be controlled by economics until after the fact, when children become expensive drains on household economies. Poor people, like the affluent, have no intention of "going away" so the world can feel more comfortable in not having to "deal" with them!

Also, there is a terrible conflict of "survival" where mass communication dangles "success images" before the hungry eyes of the perpetually "insufficient." Yet, we close entryways for adaptational potential of "foreigners" to achieve affluence. This produces community inhabitants who (a) symbolically "act out" aggression at personal or property "symbols" of their deprivation, (b) utilize violent forms of problem-solving to "dramatize" depressing life scenarios, and (c) display the only type of definitive power at their disposal. Violent crimes, terrorist attacks, aggressive use of automobiles, weaponed resistance of police detention, vandalism, rape, disorderly conduct and other forms of physical destruction are cultivated "naturally" in a receptive host environment. These circumstances devastatingly impact surrounding atmospheres where power is symbolized by economic wherewithal, intellectual skills, access to jurisprudential process and litigation, physical health and nutrition, cultural opportunity, etc. The affluent become inadvertent victims of various expressions of psychosocial despair and alienation, of which all of us are a participatory component.

3. *Cultural Creativity:* The loss we all experience when large numbers of human minds and talents, spiral into darkened caverns of inactivity, boredom, depression, malaise, irrelevance, and degenerative stagnation; is obviously difficult to measure. We *do* know, however, the enjoyment and spirit-elevating pleasure we *have* received from creative writers, musicians, composers, actors, artists, dancers, audiovisual engineers, horticulturists, architectural designers and a host of other performers and artisans. In this regard, we should reasonably extrapolate that contributions from increasing percentages of the populace would certainly improve and expand the overall quality of cultural life.

   Creativity, and human energy, applied to challenging tasks of industrial and agricultural development, should also contribute to greater abundance for everyone. This would result in fewer unproductive "dependents" as rising middle-class groups decrease the birthrate and produce expansion of leisure time for everyone. These benefits could be utilized reciprocally to develop each citizen's personal talent and creative capacity. Movement toward a worldwide, but conservatively affluent, "middle class" will become even more necessary in the future:

   a. Technology will decrease jobs directly applied to production, so that poverty-stricken numbers will *increase* to the point of saturation of funds and programs to control aggression and "manage" their survival.

   b. The world will become a leisure culture where basic survival is insured. Most life agendas will be spent in development of spiritual and aesthetic pursuits for enlightenment of the soul in the well-fed body. Everyone needs to intellectually and socially prepare, now, to accommodate this style of living.

c. Middle-class "deferred gratification norms" will become mandatory to decrease population, to insure comfortable survival within the "emerging" scope of space-age technology.

d. Medical technology will prolong life almost indefinitely, so human resource "compatibility" will become increasingly necessary.

e. Expanding international markets, plus consolidation of multicultural mega-corporations, will demand substantial leveling and balancing of intellectual, social, behavioral, and emotional traits. This will insure mutuality and harmonious interaction between formerly divergent cultural factions and competitive capital philosophies.

f. Decreased demands on mental and emotional activity to "simply survive" will stimulate extensions of psychic powers into metaphysics, religion, spirituality, emotionality, etc. Human compassion, personal growth, and social justice will "probably" become central concerns of large numbers of people who will not need to "worry and work" to survive.

g. Third World nations will obtain nuclear/technical power as a threat to world stability, and less populated middle-class nations will be forced to reconcile the existence of incredible numbers of impoverished peoples. They will insist on recognition and will "back up" formerly idle threats to peace.

4. *Metaphysical Stimulation:* There is little doubt of the extreme social impact of increasing "extra-," "ultra-," "sub-," "transcendent," "ulterior," "supra-," etc. sensory and neuro-cognitive/biologic perception and ecologic interaction between various *life forms* and *energy sources*. This "inclusive" need suggests considerable personal loss in maintenance of subcultural idiographic concepts, beliefs, and "mind-bending" mental preoccupations of "sameness" (the self seeing itself as consistent, and other "selves" as different-to-be-excluded-from-oneness or from shared consciousness). There is little value in excluding vast riches of cogito-psychic stimulation and nurturance, which para-psychologic researchers tell us exist *between* "energizing" organisms that *remove* artificial blockages to a vast matrix of interconnective alliances. Most "affluents" expend excessive effort to deny failure scripts and characteristics we fear in *our* vulnerable selves. We employ commensurate mental gymnastics to consolidate differential values, to convince ourselves of our middle-class relevance. The difference we thus exaggerate is an illusion: dead people may be dressed differently, but the absence of either "sophisticated" or "primitive" thought in decayed

neurons still equals zero, no matter how large the qualitative cultural index was the instant before death. Discriminative personal and cultural differentiation wastes time and energy which might be spent in the following ways:

a. knowing the "whole self," rather than the half which is "leftover" after we scapegoat the vulnerable/fearful image in the persona of life's "losers";

b. knowing other people whose "differentiated" image may be the "lost" part of our selves that can complete the holistic puzzle of internal emotional life;

c. expanding awareness of collective conscious forces that stimulate gaps in our own thought processes, and energize cognitions which may be trapped by our own energy-excluding isolationism;

d. uniting with a security-building network of consciousness-filling "units" of emotional life, which may improve universal problems of loneliness, isolation, fears of dependency, alienation, etc.;

e. connecting with basic "roots" of human existence, which many insist is a "circular path" that involves active and passive influences of ancestors (who may be either rich or poor), spirits of the dead or not-yet-living, selves in former and future lives, animal forms and spirits, ecologic forces and powers, God or Supernatural influences, and universal "energy systems";

f. enriching emotions and perceptual horizons by "tuning in" to awarenesses of people with different cultural experiences to "feel and understand" the full range of "comprehensive humanity";

g. "joining mental forces" with global humanity to resolve common problems, "right" disparate fear-based conceptions, and decrease conflict with alienated and "enemy" cultures (e.g., the harmonic convergence).

5. *Spiritual Humanity:* Several *fundamental principles* are noticed with women and men involved in psychotherapeutic pursuits of freedom from "dependencies" (guilt, anger, compulsion, boredom, anxiety, psycho-physiologic illness, fear) that "regress" us to childhood conflicts. These regard "spiritual" and emotional "menus" that are explored, created, revised, expanded, contracted, and intermittently validated by people from all cultural heritages throughout various stages of their lives. The following

truths are observed by "digging" inside the mind to pare away encrusted defenses which limit the full realization of every human soul:

a. Everyone passionately hungers to be "legitimated" as a valuable "feeling" individual for the "self," and at least one other human.

b. Everyone harbors fear that they will "fail," and believes strongly in personal "success" as one avenue to "actualization and victory" for the spiritual or emotional personality.

c. Everyone perceives an intensified "electrical" linkage between humans, or within specific life circumstances, which is not always explainable. It represents for them, evidence of "life-bonding" between human minds, hearts, spirits, biologies, etc.

d. Everyone supports intrinsic freedom of choice and expanded opportunity as a cornerstone of "qualitative social life." They unequivocally resent external (and internal, although this takes longer in therapy to discover) situational constraints or structural limitations on the "choosing" and "being" process.

e. Everyone (although sometimes obscured from self-awareness) seeks "ultimate fulfillment" of human destiny relative to other beings. Each participant, wants to "influence" or exert benevolent "power" to assist other individuals to be happier, feel "better," reduce negative emotions, achieve success, etc.

f. Everyone believes that results of constructive or destructive action are "registered" *somewhere* within a higher, superordinate framework or "domain" of "qualitative essence." This reciprocally serves as a stimulus and rationale for either performing or emotionally supporting (even if this is a very private or "secret" experience) good deeds and humanitarian affections.

g. Everyone has cried in some symbolic or real way, over human "pain." We all "understand," at least once in life, the horrible degradation, despair, and uselessness of perpetual suffering, regardless of who the sufferer happens to be.

h. Everyone has creative and useful ideas, with significant applications regarding major areas of human-caused alienation and unproductive/ destructive social process. These ideas apply to (1) bureaucratic organizational inefficiency, (2) lack of motivation and enthusiastic participation, (3) starvation, illness, overcrowding, community development, (4) war and international conflict, (5) governmental integrity and facilitative helpfulness, (6) interpersonal conflict resolution and problem-solving, (7) development and maintenance of human creativity, (8) satisfying recreation and entertainment needs, (9) effective and qualitative child-rearing, (10) the beauty and value of human "love."

i. Everyone experiences elation, or satisfaction, when a more "capable" individual or force "expresses itself" to rescue a "victim" of greater vulnerability or weakness. We emote when we protect a less fortunate, naive, helpless or dependent individual or animal from danger caused by destructive power, or from isolating exclusion from a deserved status of recognition and respect.

j. Everyone understands and, to some degree, appreciates the functional value of independent/dependent "reciprocity" in social interactions. We know that "something of value" can be "given" and "received" by every living creature. We frequently "feel" that the highest degree of qualitative life emanates from a *balance* between these factors.

Given "commonalities" in the repertoire of *every* life, the conclusion that we are "destined," or have a "learned" mission to assist less fortunate "brothers and sisters," in a world-culture, appears quite obvious. This conclusion seems justified because an extraneous and theoretical value exhorts us to "be humane," as this "energy of compassionate living" exists, somewhere, in everyone. The astute reader, of course, will retort that "buried humanistic treasure" under the protective armor of "insensitive materialists," within a culture overburdened with inflexible organizational and procedural structure—contraindicates idealistic pleas for more caring. Citizens can consider, however, that most of our daily "material" and "pragmatic" attentions may really represent diversions, defenses, detours, or misrepresentations of a genuinely central focus of "interpersonal synergy," which most of us search for within ancillary "tributaries" of differentiated social life. We experience "specialness," additionally, as a profound "moving" awareness during particular peak periods of development, when crises have reduced our defenses, or in response to affective stimuli which remind us of the core of life we share.

As life paths and illusory "divine idols" lead to impoverished or sterile results in the insatiable search for "existential relevance," maybe the only approach is to decide whether the depths of inter-human attachment and shared energy provide a warmer feeling, than other less "humanitarian" outcomes. We might use this comparative observation to consider even greater "gains" in exposing ourselves to the levels of *nonhuman* deprivations within the culture of poverty.

Conclusion and Recommendations

The last section of this chapter is, perhaps, the most important. It offers particular ways to confront and ameliorate, even to a small extent, the horrible conditions of poverty, drug abuse, and crime. Everyone will not adopt each strategy, and each reader may "engage" the challenge at different levels of involvement and energy. In any event, I hope everyone explores at least one option, if not for your own benefit, then to help those who desperately cry out for the assistance and strength:

Option #1: Organize Volunteers

There is considerable need among poor and poverty (not "stricken") "cultural" habitats, for services, consultations and learning opportunities which are (a) beyond the scope and limited resources of human service agencies, (b) lost within intergovernmental organizational structures designed to "manage" rather than "improve" situations, and (c) considered too costly by "upper-class" policymakers and commercial capitalist enterprises to which the "haves" pay allegiance. These services are now most efficiently delivered outside the "confines" of "eviscerative" agency structures and philosophic premises, which are conservatively "vested" social welfare programs. Private citizens, with combined economic resources, can establish direct liaisons with individuals, families or leaders in poor communities to address "specific" needs for: literacy education, health care, family planning, home repair, employment preparation, child care, legal advice, accessing community resources, emergency food and shelter, or advocacy. Social agencies should welcome concerned citizens with interest to work directly with those "in need." If approached with respect and non-diminutive authority, most of those who need economic, consultative or physical assistance will accept thankfully. Volunteers must remember that generations of negative experience will not reverse immediately, and helpers should develop patience, and expect regressions on the road to equality.

Option #2: Alert the Media

Sensationalistic "tragedies" and successes are commonly sought by magazine, T.V., radio, or newspaper reporters to "stimulate" constituencies and boost Arbitron (Fake-a-tron, Dope-a-tron, Waste-a-tron) ratings. Concomitantly, there is little longitudinal or in-depth interest among media sponsors to reveal *comprehensive* pictures of the ugly side of beautiful contemporary life. We also become "confused" within a maze of "seemingly" complicated causes, solutions, and organizations. Media serve an important function to "transport" fearful people away from "realizations" of life's basest experiences, so that dreams are perpetuated to the advantage of all who seek ultimate relevance. Media abandon comprehensive social problems when marketing enterprises augment product sales by associating salable items with "elevated" principles of human ascension, pleasure, freedom, etc. These concerns, unfortunately, are not "rubricked" among the classes of "have nots," except in romanticized myth.

Mainstream publics, however, must be "inundated with the truth" of classism and categorically restricted access to all dimensions of the good life. Citizens should pressure local and national media programmers to concentrate "scrutinizing lenses" on the tragedies which simultaneously counterbalance, yet "represent" assumed qualities of illusorily inverted "essences of humanity." Messages will eventually be "heard" and respected by media and sponsors, once the focus of competition turns from fantasy to reality. In this context, audiences are "taught" about their responsibility for continuation of "wastes" which impact us all.

Option #3: Lobby Political Leaders

Although governmental spending does not represent the totality of economic "energy" in the world, considerable dollars are wasted on irrelevant grant projects with peripheral quality-of-life outcomes. Excessive monies are gobbled-up in projects which directly or indirectly *contribute* to potentials for human destruction (weapons systems, military operations, covert-government aggressive incantations, ultra-lethal high-technology anti-organismic substances, etc.). Otherwise "productive" capital for industry, cultural advancement, or specific subgroup rehabilitation is also subterfuged or dwindled away in cost-inefficient mismanagement of bureaucratic systems. Although Congress-people must be responsive to special interests of "relevant" constituencies representing broad bases of national survival (we *cannot* abandon industry, obviously), everyone is aware of exorbitant profits gained by a select minority of influential entrepreneurs. Money *not* spent on poverty programs is also money equally stolen from the middle classes, who also are not privileged to share in top-level profits. In fact, middle income individuals and families lose money because the taxable mainstream citizen, not corporate enterprise, pays the bill for welfare, where too little is spent, and too much "cream" is diverted to the top.

Although most readers of this book will never "own" a senator, representative, governor, etc., we all can prevent acquisition of elected office by irresponsible legislators through the inexpensive and uncomplicated voting procedure. Letters, phone calls, group or association letters of support, campaign assistance—followed by "poverty-sensitive" votes—*can* make a difference!

Option #4: Form Alliances with Industry

The capital to provide adequate sustenance to all citizens must presently come from profit-yielding investments by industry. This satisfies mass-demand human need by stimulating work energy applied to conversion of "inert" or unusable resources, to produce commodities that feed, clothe, shelter citizenry. "Productions" also satisfy aesthetic needs which are "mandated" by symbolizing minds in need of stimulation and beliefs of personal value (justification/ compensation for human pain or suffering). Industry or productive human service (which emerges in highly technologized societies) is the foundation for sustenance of the "vulnerable human mentality," regardless of whether the econo-political philosophy is capitalism, communism, or socialism. In this context, "social activists" for the poor will get nowhere in adversarial debate about materialistic insensitivity of "big business." Business holds the "trump card" for social policies (although competition provides "checks and balances" to discourage ultimate "checkmate" of government by managers of production), and has little reason to be threatened by social ideology. Secondly, business will not be deeply intimidated, because operating profits are desperately needed for investment into all unproductive regions of social life. Therefore business must be "courted" to understand advantages of socially conscious/economically strategic attention to the poor. Readers may become active in developing the following:

a. "expansion plans" for businesses which include property relocations in depressed areas (lower operating costs);

b. profiles of expanded markets for specific products through capital investment of jobs for the poor, who create production energy plus reciprocal "consumer dependency";

c. holistic education programs to help leaders in industry understand (1) direct losses of "undersocialized" employees, or peripheral losses of undeveloped markets, and (2) general social deterioration/disruption caused by increasing numbers of poverty victims of work-productivity age levels (e.g., the deep-seated conflict between rich and poor castes in an unstable Middle East that explodes into worldwide markets, causes enormous losses of oil profits, and is labeled, incorrectly and perniciously, by despotic leaders as a "political" problem);

d. political values of public philanthropy for truly deprived audiences, whereby alterations of *extreme* levels of deprivation, represent a greater ratio of secondary advantage to business, as opposed to smaller increments of improvement for other beneficiaries who begin higher on the need scale, and "move" lesser distance; or

e. investment of profits in "human potential," (management long-term commitments to future employees recruited from workers with more modest means, than the demanding workers from mainstream classes, which may produce enhanced motivation, as well as job competition to begin de-escalations of exorbitant wages, etc.).

Option #5: Advocate Stringent Anti-Crime Philosophies

The gross-deprivational atmosphere of poverty or *near-poverty* produces an unstable and untrusting childhood environment. Parental frustrations and fears cumulatively turn into grotesque forms of irresponsibility, neglect, displaced anger, ambivalence, reactive delusions of self-importance, impulsiveness, punitive expressions of pseudo-power, or self-centered manipulativeness and dishonesty. The existence of these "justifiable defenses" among role models, and the virtual impossibility of correcting ingrained patterns of "necessary adaptation," does not dismiss the undeniable *fact* that "personalities" are "created" at a very young age. They are supported throughout adulthood, and are "pathogenic" and mentally-socially indexed for chronic participation in crime, drug abuse, and perpetual social irresponsibility. Masses of personalities with underdeveloped and maturationally-distorted pathologies of "character," cannot be reversed or substantially altered by therapy, adult education, imprisonment (which reinforces negative self-perceptions and social resentment, while also fulfilling dependency and external control "needs"), behavior modification techniques, or modest attempts at neighborhood rehabilitation and community organization. These techniques do not work because of the following: (a) basic perceptions are permanently "seeded" in fundamental formulas of the "self"; (b) the need for cultural consonance and familiarity, pressures "social deviants" to repeatedly return to their "natural" environments—which do not change; and (c) the world "sponsors" egalitarian values and mediates contingent associations between differentiated social classes relative to power of controlling elitists, as a matrix of conflicting ideologies which are manipulated by the "haves," at the expense of the "have nots." Attempts to correct cultures of poverty and their subsidiary manifestations must begin predominantly with younger generations of children growing into a new atmosphere. Simultaneously, negative adult influences must be permanently removed or otherwise controlled within existing or transforming community conditions. Actions necessary, therefore, for the layperson or professional, relative to crime and drugs, are these:

a. Citizens must pressure legislatures and courts to adopt permanent and semipermanent incarceration philosophies for "chronic recidivists," and extensive incarceration/therapeutic programs for serious drug abusers. "Hardened criminals" will not change, and must be removed from the environment for the protection of "child learners" and "victims" alike. Despite enormous expense, ***humane*** conditions of lengthy isolation must be developed.

b. The extensive network of criminal systems of planning, product distribution, financing, and organized and informal operation *demands* a *comprehensive community attack,* to render a "fatal blow" of monumental proportions. Citizens should demand military, business, mental health/welfare, police, and private volunteer integration of a worldwide task force which strikes at the "strategic headquarters" of criminal and drug networks. Concurrently, permanent citizen protection is required, plus regular deterrent prohibitions in every community. Citizen special interest groups can be formed among friends, colleagues, or interested parties to write letters and lobby in city and state government, plus institute pressure thrusts at Congress to authorize expansion of police capability.

c. Citizens can foster community anti-crime/drug education programs for children as well as victims. Individual responsibility and power is required for identification of illegal activities or "perpetrators." Communities must develop personal, family and organizational defenses against victimization by criminal operations.

d. Although "people" injure or kill "other people," the massive manufacture, sale, *romanticization* and ownership of lethal weapons *must be eliminated.* Federal subsidization of weapons industries is needed to convert operations to development of "peaceful" products. Media campaigns and legislation can dissuade reliance on lethal force as a solution to problems of power equalization, anxiety reduction, and self-esteem enhancement. Weapons of destruction, have never benefitted any society longitudinally, and "hunting" values (with which I disagree) can be maintained, if desired, through state and local licensure and storage of weapons which are not in use.

Option #6: Money Donations

Waste, corruption, and inept planning have destroyed the effectiveness of model cities, community reconstruction, government subsidized housing, or other welfare programs. Discriminately and judiciously monitored donations are very appropriate and can be competently utilized by selected, specific programs which operate in every city in most countries. There are many ways to directly give, or "endow," portions of income to good programs. The consolidation of funds from private organizations or individuals, over extended numbers of years, can create and sustain comprehensive efforts to help the poor at "causal" rather than "symptomatic" levels of the problem.

Option #7: Education

The final choice for becoming more involved in the "poverty problem" is to encourage educational efforts within schools, churches, businesses, private clubs, and even groups of friends. All these organizations can help children and adults realize the "holistic" nature of this concern, which impacts everyone, and requires total community interest and energy for resolution. We all benefit by meeting "real people" who actually live with filth, starvation, fear of violence, neighborhood disorganization, abuse and neglect, poor health and health care, financial impoverishment, and numerous forms of spiritual and emotional despair. We must educate each new generation to be sensitive to, and comprehensively connected with, broad social and psycho-spiritual "essences of human reality." Citizens should monitor academic curriculum to insure that social, behavioral, ecological, human, community development, and *peace sciences* become foundations for learning and orientation for emerging adults. Informal education comes when each of us challenges friends and colleagues to think and "feel" about the poor, and action develops when we say to one another—"Let's Get Involved Now!"

Chapter III

THE ROLE OF EDUCATION IN SOCIETY TODAY

Every citizen attests to the intrinsic and functional value of "education" per se, although few analyze the philosophical premises of past, present, or future formal or informal "learning." Also, concerned adults rarely interact directly with Boards of Education, School Superintendents, Principals or even teachers in a *concerted* effort to influence "what" is taught, and "how" the product is delivered to the student. Unfortunately for the outcome of world or community events, basic processes of "reasoning" and "knowing" reality are permanently programmed into young people by the age of 10 or 12. Their subsequent applications of cognitive capabilities are, to some extent, lagging behind current circumstances to which contemporary processes of thought should be applied. In the rampaging world of techno-economic "leap-frog-to-the-hundredth-power," our "present mind-set" can change the "content" of specific *concepts* as they expand or contract to integrate newly discovered facts or principles of the universe. However, there are problems surrounding creeds which function as "berths" to shape explanations of facts, and provide diagrammatic prescriptions of "truths" explored selectively by science, which are confirmed through broad-based "implications" of data which emerge. These credos, as product, process, and purpose of culture, become cornerstones of logic, emotion, evaluation, and exploration that were cemented earlier in the histories of "current" thinking group cohorts. There is reason to doubt therefore, whether anyone views *current* material, social, or psychological reality without prepackaged "belief idiosyncracies" of parents, family, other childhood educators, or media. Children are burdened or blessed with assumptive and experiential "baggage" from one or two previous generations, and are challenged to (1) engage in learning, followed by (2) unlearning of antiquated information, followed by (3) learning to be autonomous from cultural programming to learn facts in particular ways, followed by (4) learning *new* information. What we "know" is probably yesterday's news by the time we "unhook" from the past, and tune in to the present (which races toward the future, i.e., it "becomes" even before it "is").

If we resolve issues about "where" educational values come from, or "when" they are implanted, we are left with a parallel dilemma. We must figure out *who* decides *which* values are vehicles upon which corresponding or antithetical "facts" are transported into the malleable minds of learners. Although the world will continue its incessant dialogue (actually simultaneous monologue because few people "listen" to others) about "constituent rights" to influence education; parents, teachers and students will exercise *minimal* control of curriculum in elementary, high school, or college. Politics and professional "orientations" will always intervene, and students experience open-minded education and ability to be fundamentally "changed" by learning, as extinct possibilities. As long as someone or some group decides facts and values children learn, it is certain that students will have minimal exposure to the viewpoints of the "curriculum control debate losers." They may never know the other half of the circle of "continuous knowing." This hemisphere presents an *alternate* scenario, and also serves as supportive backdrop for the prominent half of the holistic world panorama children *do* learn (a top is not a top without a bottom—which cannot be itself without a top which is not it). The only rational answers to this question of who decides what the learner learns, are (1) *everybody* decides because each person has at least one piece of the "reality puzzle" or (2) *nobody* decides and the learner explores, experiences and integrates at his/her own discretion. In any other conjecture about learning, someone "wins" and the other faction "loses," politics guide curriculum design, and students become "manipulated manikins" of various power elites.

Still further in the query is the relationship between fact ("what" is learned) and "process" ("how" we learn to learn or not learn). This connection impacts matriculating in formal educational roles, but also concerns the ways *learning* and *knowing* function in other social "processes." Observations of all levels of education, generally, reveal a "monolithic" structure which takes on the following *characteristics* relative to both content and process of learning:

1. The "process" of education is "believed" to be most fertile, *prior to the age of young adulthood*—which possibly means the following:

   a. Adults are not expected to change by re-entering the "process" of examination, confrontation, critique, or exploration developmentally (e.g., ask your employer for time off to go to school, and see what happens).

b. Education is "earmarked" for employment preparation, and maintains a narrow purview of "content" that could apply to maturational or situational learning "crises."

c. Childhood education is presumed to contain sufficiently potent "blossoming seeds" of "process" to enable learners who survive, to activate opportunities for growth as subsequent needs or situations dictate.

d. Education is philosophically viewed as a strong correlate to economic productivity and physical subsistence. Higher levels of spiritual or intellectual development throughout the life span are subordinate concerns relative to advanced "job" training or personalized education "on one's own time."

e. Education is subsumed as socializational development of children, and does not appear an appropriate "expectation" for adults.

f. "Basic content" of knowledge is considered to be relatively standardized, as is the "process" of "thinking," so that fundamental "levels" can be taught in one early "block" of instruction. Subsequent embellishment is considered an addendum to "foundation" theories of "what" and "how."

g. Education of children serves a range of societal functions, not exclusively educational. They include control and management to assist parents, removal of labor competition, provision of occupational opportunities for teachers (e.g., women who compete for male jobs), etc.

2. Most traditional curricula are *"content" oriented* to accomplish the following:

a. Content provides basic skills related to physical survival at extremely elementary levels (e.g., reading, writing, arithmetic);

b. Content teaches culture-bound "truths" to produce "conformity" to econo-centric practices of "production," and insure mainstream adaptation to "social orders" designed to provide workers and consumers for production "orientations";

c. Content inculcates elementary principles of logical, deductive, linear, materialistic and positivistic reasoning as "life explanation" frameworks (for Western industrial nations particularly) to insure intra-cultural harmony, and reduce anxiety-producing "black holes" in "consistent" ideology;

d. Content reinforces conformity and dependence on authority through "content regurgitation," and delivery of content within pedagogical styles of transference from superior to inferior.

3. *Content,* intra-structurally, is generally *conservative* and *constricted* to the extent that:

   a. Perspectives of social "majorities" predominate because:

      (1) these people write the textbooks,

      (2) they provide the consumer market for the media which tell them about themselves and that they are "OK,"

      (3) society's patterns of capitalistic property and business ownership, market exploitation, materialistic and spiritual "productivity" philosophies, middle-class social affluence, and international imperialism are most supportive of conservative general public mentalities,

      (4) "conforming" and "justifying" viewpoints are least likely to create dissonance among emerging opinionated adolescents and their "mainstream" parents, and

      (5) conservative explanations produce the greatest degrees of perceived and actual social "harmony" among delicately balanced competitive social groups and competing parts of each cognitive "self."

   b. "Public" education exists in a world filled with vulnerable and frightened social and psychological "animals," who generally refuse to admit ignorance of the "meaning of life." The herd postulates special interest group "truths" to insure coalition of "likes" and separation of "differents." They therefore, *mediocritize* a "middle of the road vanilla" perspective (which may be no perspective at all) to avoid offending taxpayers who pay educators' salaries (maybe to "not educate").

   c. Liberalized differentiation of viewpoints rapidly demolishes ideologic "myths" which hold society together. Exploration finds "gaps and holes" (discrepancies, exceptions and falsehood) in "rational" thought and primary value positions. Classroom "evaluative honesty" provides an arena to experience "conflict" of interpersonal belief, which looms as a serious threat to "crowd control." Students with time, energy, and "freshness" of vision can seriously disrupt "orderly" social frameworks.

d. Conservative curricula protects teachers from embarrassment related to their ignorance (which is expected with low salaries, difficult job responsibilities, and inferior educational standards) of multiple levels of topic analysis, or highly specialized aspects of any one subject.

4. *"Processes"* of learning, thinking, feeling, deciding, etc. are possibly *neither taught nor* analytically *experienced,* except in very unique courses. Emphasis on "how" rather than "what," is limited by parochialism of "theory and philosophy," and fixed "content perspective," which represents "truth" to be absorbed by the learner. Other "process-related" issues, however, are these:

   a. We need to help students learn "who" they and others "think" they "are," how people choose and maintain identities, and what functions mental processes serve in life. This teaching requires expertise in philosophy, psychology, sociology, history, ethics and logic, etc., which (1) is beyond the scope of educators not rewarded for specialization in "soft" sciences, (2) represents "generalist" theory which creates public skepticism about mitigated competence, and (3) violates norms advocating "pragmatic" education for economic, rather than psycho-spiritual "survival."

   b. Teaching "process" results in few "definitive answers," and often raises more questions. These become frightening and frustrating for a citizenry interested in showcasing practical "outcomes" of educational expenses. Process educating exacerbates psychic discomfort among parents, teachers, administrators and community leaders who want to appear "solid" in philosophical beliefs, and avoid struggles with their own "relativity and validity" demons.

   c. Teaching process exposes historical facts to analytic scrutiny, where (1) "end vs. means" issues easily deflate nationalistic heroic "image mirages," (2) cognitive dissonance is created for all who support (directly or indirectly) the status quo of federal governments/religious sects/hereditary cultural groups, (3) concepts of human "superiority" are prostrated to a much "baser" realm of the "hedonistic animal world."

d. Experiencing "process" necessitates removal of intellectual defenses of concept symbolization and projection. Students are forced to discuss themselves and each other very unguardedly, and cannot escape painful issues of life (and death) by focusing on content topics that remain "out there" someplace.

Another question about education within communities, concerns its role within the "politics" of *social stratification:*

1. "Education" has evolved throughout history as one of several *differentiating attributes* to identify *"status" hierarchies* of social groups. Distinction between those possessing knowledge and information, and their "deficit plagued" community counterparts, evolutionally constituted "natural selection cut-off points." "Ignorance" represented those who could not survive ecological demands for hunting, fishing, food gathering, planting, protection from predators, and avoidance of incompatible environmental elements. With human "techno-production" advancement, however, numerically larger civilizations reduced life/premature death ratios. The mind's search for greater stimulation and challenge was "unleashed" from basic subsistence worries during increasing leisure time. Simultaneously, the mind discovered that one of several major "corridors" of possibly infinite levels of "ascending adequacy" was the mind's *view-of-itself,* relative to "concept manipulation and idea retention."

   "Expansiveness" of mental "operations" is an excellent escape route from children's dependency on parents, because it is private/secret, and not easily identified for "jealous retaliation." The open-ended mind inversely counteracts corresponding deprivation, relative to physical constraints imposed by authority (physical characteristics of life, are converted to ideologic counterparts as children and culture grow).

   The emergent division of labor in complex societies, required to organize sequential task operations for "production," does not *necessarily* imply a status hierarchy of differential knowledge and learning. Every "job" can simply be subdivided into larger or smaller "categories" or symbolic abstractions of its essence or nature. Human need for psychologic security (tension reduction, absence of pain, etc.), however, when "extrapolated" into the social world as competition for "scarce resources," becomes transformed into comparisons of various "units of knowledge." This happens when survival "matures" from issues of acquisition of food and shelter, to concepts of "earned remuneration" within industrial money exchange economies. Control of money (symbolized biologic need-meeting resources) and property, then, become "sacred tabernacles" of one's secure and relevant identity. This occurs against the background of worldwide systems of production, consumption, and "entrepreneurialism." Amount or type of knowledge, therefore, become criteria to wrestle authority and control away from anticipated "predators," who, paradoxically, are needed to assist in production and to remain loyal "consumers." In this context of interdependency, knowledge becomes differentiated into various levels of theoretical abstraction and discipline "variability." This facilitates comprehensiveness in "strategic" planning, plus "precision" craftsmanship for production. Knowledge becomes an "exonerative imprimatur" for "transmogrified vulnerability" in the form of discriminated social roles which provide security to all who conform to "between" and "within" role expectations.

Smaller units of culture, find themselves "outgunned" by community organizations and public service operations that support agriculture and industry, provide basic services, and control cultural deviation. Families, as one example, discover the "transcendent functions" of ethno-centric knowledge and learning. Each family becomes "special" (valid, relevant, secure) by "knowing" unique facts and ways of thinking and evaluating, that support its experienced "avenues of access" into the production/consumption maze of operations and organizations. Successive generations give retrospective validation to the significant needs of ancestors, and families boost collective esteem relative to other families, through boundary-fortifying functions of differentiated knowledge.

2. A second role for education socioculturally, is a *massive form of absolution,* amnesty, indemnity, pacification and propitiation. It explains everything that "goes wrong," both accidentally and purposefully, within the production-consumption scenario for world survival. Education is the "cumulative integration" of concrete concepts (symbols of external reality), formed into "sets" of interactive cause and effect stimuli. These outcomes are presumed (agreed to by norms of social groups) to result in "conditions" of qualitative "being" of the person-within-the-situation. Concrete ideas become "action agents" to influence one another because of "higher" level abstract symbols (constructs). With their elevated theoretical status, these principles "transcend" the physical limitations of reality (especially components of identity). Therefore, they create "attributes of association" between representations which do not *literally* exist anywhere as empirical atoms or molecules (or other *material* "forms"). They are, however, fabricated to enable otherwise unnatural, artificial or complex interweaving of antithetical, dissonant or diametric "phenomena." They "appear" to fit together in some form of "harmonious totality." Consequences of conceptual or action *conflictual* linkages are subsumed within a "reasonable-

appearing umbrella ideology" so that "traces" of their former anomalous existence seem to "make sense" (e.g., religious wars, growth following economic depression, physical abuse [spanking] of children, state lotteries in non-gambling states, etc.).

Given the enormously "free" latitude of idea creation and utilization, the person "with" knowledge is dangerous because they possess an arsenal of cognitive skills to maneuver "logic." As this capability "matures," almost anything can "seem" justified if the right "variables" are discovered which authorize desired conclusions. The person "without" education is equally vulnerable, because they also conceptualize within their own "ignorance" framework of how the world works. They may additionally be relegated to denial of responsibility for "knowing" (understanding and deciding) and simply respond in a physio-indulgent manner of impulsive egotism, and ignore overarching theoretical meanings of their actions.

In the above context, ideas that represent knowledge become imaginary, ghostlike apparitions, that live vicarious lives for their human "owners." "They" engage in mock battles/liaisons, etc., win/lose/go to heaven or hell, and serve as standard bearers for values, to conclude there is "significance" to time spent on what we presume to be "this earth." Whatever happens within this life space, is explained or divested of its attendant fear-inducing anxiety, with the communication, recollection, enculturation, vivication, sanctification, and "meta-mutation"-over-time of various bits and pieces of knowledge.

Knowledge has "authorized" (1) ownership of slaves and the emancipation of slaves, (2) positively viewed World War I and negatively perceived Vietnam, (3) prostitution as "illegitimate" sex and holy matrimony's conjugal recreation as legitimate sex, (4) indignation at the political assassination of President Kennedy alongside U.S. assassination plans for Fidel Castro, (5) Northern Ireland's brutal civil war nestled within loving arms of Catholic and Protestant theologies of love, (6) affluent U.S.'s abhorrent conditions of poverty-in-the-womb-of-plenty, and (7) the great victory of "Desert Storm" where Iraqi women, children, and men were losers, so the U.S. could win (oil!).

3. Thirdly, education *facilitates* social progress, although "cons" accompany many wonderful "'prose'" of the world's development. Prolific advancement of medical, communication, engineering, food production, creative art, transportation, and computer technologies, etc., has miraculously transformed and exalted the quality of life for all modern societies. Progress has even indirectly occurred for the tragically deprived, but

nevertheless progressing, "Third World" countries. Demographic and socioeconomic factors like infant mortality, life span, disease morbidity, leisure time, production efficiency, product quality, human safety records, life satisfaction indices, nutrition, and other dimensions of human functioning; attest to the undeniable benefit of cumulative knowledge-building and learning. Advantages are built through experiential "inductive" means, and via formalized deductive scientific study and mathematical experimentation. With computer retrieval of information and hypothetical manipulation of ideas, facts can be integrated into formulae for rapid association, and differential "conditions of existence" can be compared to each other in complex matrices, (e.g., multiple "correlations" and statistical analysis of "variance"). Also, data reflecting previously discovered attributes of chemical, physical, psychosocial or even spiritual properties can be mathematically "projected" with computers into future configurations. This trans-"portation," obviously, allows us to "envision" patterned change over time.

The accumulation of knowledge as a foundation for culture has, additionally, assisted in the archaeologic and anthropologic understanding of historical ancestry and origin. Psychologic and sociologic sciences have also contributed to appreciation and guidance of our individual and collective lives as members of various unique cultures. Along with biochemical contributors to woman's and man's learning about the total "self," the expanding astronomic, physics, aerospace and meteorologic disciplines will catapult earthbound inhabitants into an intergalactic wonderland of new knowledge. Simultaneously, neuro-psychic and metaphysical information enhances awareness, and stimulates exploration into nontraditional "spaces" of psycho-spiritual life.

Facts we have meticulously harvested and obsessively stored provide, in the purest sense, an accumulation of meritorious building blocks. These "geometrically" explode into increasingly "advanced" development of new concepts to symbolize formerly unknown pieces of life's systemic puzzle. Abstracted concepts that represent atomic and cellular properties of "existence" and "action" from a relatively "value-free" perspective, provide a neutral, yet extremely enlightening framework to improve "material" reality. This improvement can be measured as (1) decrease of physical pain and stress; (2) self-determined management of human energy; (3) environmental control or reactive accommodation to aversive stimuli; (4) creation of pleasurable "sensation," (5) reduction of living "costs" concerning ratio of work effort (including functional deterioration of energy sources) relative to "exchange values" of goods and services, and (6) predictability of future events. Knowledge, however, does not exist in a hermetically homogeneous and "purified" cybernetic environment. Contaminating human factors and subjective interpretations are not yet excluded. Also, facts interact only with other facts without necessarily passing through psychosocial values, which positively "index" knowledge priorities and utilization contingencies. Knowledge, for its own sake, can be innocuous at its worst, and informative at its best, if it can stand alone and justify or invalidate itself, based on its "idiographic" nature. There is a problem, however, when it is subjectively interpretated within psychodynamic frameworks of fear, vulnerability, etc. when "adjectival" attributes or hierarchical dynamics of "being or action" are attached. For example, 2 + 2 can equal 4, 8, or 0 without too much problem, although a "black" 2 relative to a "white" 2, within a culture that feels 4 is "good," or 8 is "bad," creates a knowledge subordination to social prescription. Specific "red flags," therefore when considering knowledge, learning, or education in the context of social progress, are as follows:

a. Social "progress," by definition, possesses a "future" it does not yet (or may never) "own," but relates to, as a voracious "hunger." Education, as a building process, may "outrun" the ability of culture to integrate "human" with "material" nature. Changes may ignore or even destroy our valued essences as psycho-emotional "souls."

b. Education, when viewed as a qualitative attribute of humanity, relative to quantitative accumulation of facts, may contribute "progressive" illusions of "grandeur" that actually represent ignorance, within alternative frameworks of meaning and value.

c. Education does not necessarily represent "creative" thinking or "explanatory" reasoning. Some forms of sophisticated-appearing "logic" or rhetoric therefrom, usher in "regressive" or dysfunctional learning-based decisions which may retard intended growth of culture.

d. Knowledge has, to some extent, a dynamic "life" of its own. Rigid adhesion to "scientific or empirical" edifices can lead to correct progressive conclusions, within a *limited tunnel* of highly controlled data awareness. This life force can simultaneously *exclude* nonexperimental and uncontrollable extraneous information which, if "informally" (qualitative and exploratory research) integrated into precise pathways of information development, might change the concluding "realities" altogether.

e. Scientific data related to omnipresent and "pseudo-omnipotent" capitalistic consumer profiles, is a useful guide to "productive needs" satisfaction. However, it must include information on "parameters of *relationship" between* producer and consumer, so the chicken is not always studying the egg, but someone is studying the chicken-egg relationship.

f. Education is always viewed as a valued human attribute, but also an econo-political source of "power." When fantasized in the possession of "deprived minorities," therefore, it becomes a commodity to be negotiated, bought, sold, bartered or otherwise manipulated by controlling social classes. These groups historically use education to author self-serving social progress, reap substantial material and aesthetic benefits, exclude competition for jobs and property ownership, control interpersonal association, and "feel" superior.

g. Accumulation of "amount" of facts or quantity of cognitive operations intra-neurologically, is curvilinear (increases and then decreases) relative to biological maturation and decline. Everything gained in a single mind, is also lost within this same repository of learning. This relationship, in the short run, is antithetical to culture's pattern of "progress," although longitudinally may parallel the rise and fall of various civilizations. We must be wary, therefore, of the interactive role of cultural "domain" (collective humanity) and personal selfhood (individual educated mind) in making decisions about the good, the bad, and the ugly ("make my day").

In the last analysis, education as a component of epistemology, the science of learning and knowing, must be briefly considered. "Knowing" from a developmental perspective, means that neuro-sensory "data gathering mechanisms" (eyes, ears, touch, etc.), even in the intrauterine environment, are extremely busy. They sensitively receive "cues" or stimulative inputs from the immediate ecological environment, with which each human organism interacts. This misinterpreted "passive" function can be measured with scientific devices to show that changes in the sensory world around us, correspond to associated variations in the "resting or baseline" condition of the cellular organism which we "are." Our physical self continually registers neuro-electrically "coded," but cognitively symbolic "uncoded" forms of "knowledge" about the physics that surround us. Parapsychologic, metaphysical, astro-cosmologic, geo-solar, and holo-spiritual scholars insist that human "senses," in various relationship configurations, constitute a proportioned dimension of other energy, life, communicational, spacial, etc., "domains" of ethereal micro/macro reality. *From* these influences, and into their domains, "message transmissions" continually "adjust" the system for integrated functioning, and for progressive, regressive, homeostatic, or other goals it actualizes. "Directives" for the system's energy utilization and storage, define and moderate our participation in this "Taoistic" balance of life forces.

Although metaphysical and physiologic experts, generally coincide in theories concerning purely *physical exchanges,* the metaphysicians extend the nature of person-system exchange, to "active plus passive" sending, receiving and seeking functions of physical sensors. Traditional "Western" theory, on the other hand, tends toward acceptance of "passive reception" capabilities of the human "machine," unless cognitive and symbolic thought and knowledge are included in the total picture. One advantage of metaphysics, is that analysis of system component parts is not restricted by customary definitions of boundaries of the physical self. Hard-line scientific empiricists, however, are skeptical of propositions which include highly qualitative or "esoteric" data which are utilized as the basics for metaphysical and spiritual-type paradigms. Within this framework, we may possess numerous forms of "knowing," either passively taken in by sensing devices, or procured by "aggressive physio-accumulational functions" within our physiology. These "forms" may not require corresponding symbolic awareness by "cognitive selves," or more importantly, may *not be perceived* by the human mind. Current minds may be untrained in perceiving nontraditional data, or expend effort "attending" to a limited set of information.

We may "know" a good deal physically that our minds do not know we know. If we do not think we need to know, then physical processes will act automatically or "functionally," based on correct data input. Our lives, at least physically, should be in balance. Interesting questions emerge, however, when we extend issues of knowing to the neurologic and symbolic processes of the mind. In a previous section, I discussed physiologic sensations as potentially "sufficient" holistic forms of knowing/experiencing, which our minds may not, or need not, "know" about, for life to be "complete." As we grow, these sensations are "total" or "partial" (probably not "irrelevant") aspects of either the (1) person-within-environment, (2) environment-within-person, (3) environment = person, or (4) person/environment-within-something-else domains of universal existence. These experiences (true or false) are *defined* and *interpreted* by conscious and unconscious minds within the context of symbolic images. These images develop (1) *autonomously* as mind interacts directly with body, and (2) *dependently* as we apply socially ratified labels to all physiologic and material "experiences." Some theorists, of course, believe that "authentic" and direct "actualization" of the self comes through unconditioned and unfiltered connections between our minds, bodies, and external ecology. Many believe these are referent images which exist primarily in the unconscious, or momentarily in conscious minds within gaps or "free awareness spaces." These occur *between* thoughts, and are not "contaminated" by grammatical or syntactical metaphors or analogues, which limit "essences" through reductionistic "associations" to antecedent material objects (e.g., a cloud is *like* a fluffy cotton ball, white paint spot, smoke, etc.). In this case, most of us probably do not "know" much, or what we know, we do not know for very long. Our minds are trained and programmed to concentrate on practical and socially acceptable images (Don't daydream! or Pay attention!). These foci may represent "artificial" or second/third tier "knowing," which is subjective and relative to individual needs and cultural norms.

We are also *dependent* on culture to provide systems of taxonomy (naming) and rhetoric (influential communication and language). Through these, our minds "know," and we attain various levels of proficiency in "regurgitating" the range of symbols (concepts) which are provided. Increases in conceptual divisions of the holistic (if it is whole?) and otherwise undifferentiated plane of universal "is-ness" (reality or essence), however, may reverse the process of knowing the "truth." Reversal occurs through graduated mitigation of inversely increasing adjectival modifiers, which build a superstructure of vertical filters through which the initial essence is "seen." We believe we "know" the object of interest by knowing attributes of other external metaphorically symbolized "objects." *We* place these references on the path-to-awareness to "refine" the ultimate intended version. However, we may actually distance ourselves from our knowing targets. This happens the more "precisely" (micro or macro directions) we differentiate this object *from* other objects (to "know" it directly), by using other objects (with their own "idiographies") as consonant or dissonant referents. Conversely, we may know more "completely and thoroughly," in direct proportion to the categorical and attributional subdivisions which are applied to any experience. "Culture-grounded" concepts, however, trap us relative to a finite set of variables. These definitional vectors intersect to transfix the object of knowing in a relatively invariable "position," which must reflect and reciprocally validate the external concepts which are used to describe it.

Knowing, additionally, suggests a complex process of memory "implants" of past experiences, to assimilate new exposure to the "elements." It may also represent reiteration of past "functional patterns" of images within a secure cybernetic system of self-absorption. This suggests we "knew" something about reality at one or several critical "learning junctures" throughout our maturational history. We also, recurrently, "confirm past reality" to reinforce stability as the "baseline condition" of the psyche. We re-believe what we already believe, even if these concepts are renamed, and we illude they are "different." Another possibility is that new "knowing" actually occurs incrementally, but only during periods of crisis or disequilibrium. At these junctures, we "divide images," or are forced by environmental discontinuities which contradict our ideologic framework for existence, to seek new data to fill gaps in explanations. In either case, knowing represents an intermittent progressive/regressive pattern, or a crisis/stability ratio of comfortable-to-uncomfortable images (and vice versa), concerning "validity" of perceived truths. We should examine the possible impossibility of ever truly moving ahead, while tightly bound by traditions, language, shared symbols, enculturated concepts, etc. which "tell us what to believe we know," and how to manipulate data (old or new) as confirmational. Experimenters of LSD and other chemical "stimulants," noted protuberantly in the 1960s and early '70s, supported cultural and personality "enslavement" theorems. They advocated the drug experience or sensory deprivation environment as the only situation where socially conditioned mental concept-models are artificially eliminated or blocked by chemical actions. Otherwise constricted neurologic capabilities can be freed thereby, to travel their own unencumbered experiential paths. Opponents, obviously, argue that chemical inducements constitute aberrant "metabolic readjustments" which are simply pseudo knowing, even though social guideposts are unavailable for attaching "unnatural" experiences to similar natural, previously-perceived, or symbolized sensations.

From a practical standpoint, most of us will not obsess over the intricate meanings of knowing as active/passive, past/present, true/false, conditioned/natural, etc.; but we might consider the process by which beliefs of right/wrong, good/bad, beautiful/ugly, success/failure, etc., are formulated and utilized. This is necessary because we fashion complicated life scenarios around sets of knowledge which we feel are correct, helpful, and need-meeting. "Unpleasant" experiences we encounter therefore, may be directly related to (1) "facts we think we know," (2) conflictual "facts which we do not want to know," or (3) facts that tell us what and how we change, alter, manipulate, accept, reject, venerate, or modify, the foundation facts we believe represent knowledge.

In concluding this chapter, there are a number of suggestions for *all* citizens concerned about formal and informal "education," learning, or knowledge-"building" in society. These represent specific role behaviors and attitudes, which contribute to cultural, family and personal norms we utilize as foundation principles for "healthy living."

Principle #1: Pursue self-education continually and open-mindedly with an appreciation that comprehensive understanding combats alienation from the self, the world, and other people. Enhance self-confident reduction of ego-defenses, which are delusional "dramatic scripts" that reduce options for adapting and feeling "competent." Specifically pursue the following goals:

a. Study topics with which we disagree, and learn the rationale and unique circumstances which support alternate "truths."

b. Vigorously challenge the credibility of our ideologic and experiential beliefs. Learn under which existential world, cultural, community, family or personal circumstances our "trues" would become "false."

c. Think hard about the innermost nature of "facts" and value "assumptions." Consider the "soft vs. hard" realities they symbolize, and the life decisions they authorize temporarily or permanently.

d. Consider psychic constrictions and social entrapments which accompany knowledge-building that is extremely specialized, or are selected because of their enjoyable, familiar, comfortable, easy or highly individualized "nature."

Principle #2: Regularly assume postures of "no thought," to reduce stress caused by obsessively "speeding" mental "work." Control neurotic utilization of "controlled-minimum-loss," "secret-maximum-ideologic-gain," or "sacrificial moderate gain" formulas, which function only to reconcile childhood history. Expose ever-searching minds or souls to unaccustomed "communicational inputs" from other realms of our physical/spiritual selves, or from life energies elsewhere in the universal cosmos:

a. "Relax" ritualized patterns of "knowing" (thinking) which build on each other in a continuous stream of "doing." These compulsions distract the mind from overwhelming fears of the unknown "nothingness" between thoughts.

b. Consider that "non-knowing" vs "knowing" conditions of *being* are equally valid or irrelevant. These constitue evaluative perspectives to balance pursuits of "adequacy," where the knowing process illustrates the accepted cultural vehicle to "go somewhere in life."

c. Appreciate control we can exercise over the existence, nature, energy, tempo, positioning, etc. of *thought,* by experimenting with dissolution of specific knowledge themes ("distrust" of blacks only exists when we "think" it). Cognitive creations and manipulations of symbols, "become" or "abdicate" reality status upon our command.

Principle #3: Examine "intrinsic" characteristics of past knowledge, which represent "solidified constructs" to define attributes or "deficits" of our "selves." These represent perceptions of stable vs. changing dimensions of the external world ecology. Particularly become cognizant of philosophical issues about how the personality or community achieve an "identity" relative to knowledge-stored-in-memory-banks. Explore *if,* and *how,* the self can change with infusion of new knowledge.

a. Realize "concretized" images of a "corporeal self," serve as the "collection basket" for inputs from others or alienated parts of our own minds (He hurt my "feelings," I "am wrong" for feeling angry). Distinct pieces of stored knowledge (individual thoughts) of "who" we are, coalesce with a seemingly "real nature" that can be "hurt, rejected, loved, attacked," etc.

b. Learn the "process" by which values grew from disparate and otherwise disconnected "facts known" by others (predominantly parents) or experiences of our physical "machinery." Realize the process differentiates ourselves from others, defines "right from wrong," etc. under the assumption that knowledge of the symbol or word (e.g., "good") creates the "essence" of the otherwise unobservable phenomenon.

c. Decide if there are occasions where past knowledge ceases to exist as a useful guideline for the present. Test the quality of personal information-gathering and decision-making to determine if you miss out on current truths, because of outdated attachments to deceased ideas.

d. Uncover the nature and extent of your "unconscious knowledge," and seek awareness of the relationship between conscious and unconscious. "Knowledge" we do *not* focus on, exercises major influences on "coded" behaviors with others. Transformed unconscious images, variously mitigate the fullest quality of closeness or satisfaction we could derive from life and its relationship options.

Principle #4: Be aware of multiple "interfacings" with communicational messages from written, verbal, auditory, or visual media sources. These represent "survival-needing" organizations or associations of people who market their own "products" (goods or services). We do this for compensation, or to acquire/solicit reception of profit-bearing "outputs" from others (which is also a power interchange for the consumer who sells their "need"). Become cognizant of the ways knowledge is used to "control" perceptions of human "states of being" ("You *need* a new car"). Understand procedures that *manipulate* (current education) consumers or producers to exchange compensation (usually money, labor energy, appreciative service reception) relative to future action (". . . and in order to have your new car, you should sign a contract today at Hunk O'Junk Motors").

a. Be aware of the world's believed mandate to "name" or "rename" the truth in order to define life-satisfaction or need-deprivation with "attributions" of "action-energies." Refuse to be "taught" what others decide you (and your children) "should" know or "do," to fit in or become fulfilled.

b. Search for "facts" to support "revelations" of reality. Help those you encounter realize that states of "knowing" (being educated) with insufficient or false supportive information, build pyramids of delusional security.

They ultimately shift and crumble, because incorrect knowledge bumps into accurate assertions of correct knowing. Restless minds routinely change paradigms of known beliefs for no other reason than to combat boredom and extend aspirations of progressive life journeys (e.g., it will either be cloudy or sunny, and if either condition lasts too long we will inevitably alter its "essence"). Communicate that one of the most profound states of "knowing" is *honestly* "not knowing."

c. Assess your behavior patterns, and antecedent "believed values" which are conditioned (stimulus-response chain of learning) by "carrots" enticingly extended, or threateningly removed by other communicators. Often, the full extent of knowledge is not presented to help us see the comprehensive pattern of interaction, as longitudinal profile. Frequently events are isolated to justify the beliefs of others, by causing *us* to behave in ways to reinforce *their* beliefs. Also, critical opportunities for education are excluded because of self-serving needs of those who control information-disseminating media. This scenario appears in international politics, where one government ignores its perpetrated atrocities on other countries (always for *"honorable"* reasons, of course) to highlight "justifiable retaliation" based on what appears to be an autonomous stimulus from an "enemy." This monotonous chain only ends with one government disengaging totally from the game, or initiating an exclusively positive stimulus with no strings attached.

Principle #5: Consider the role you might play as an advocate for "adult education" at every level of social life. This includes (1) innovative discovery; (2) appreciation of "theoretical" dimensions of adult developmental and maturational stages, needs and crises; and (3) encouragement of other adults and "educating" institutions (colleges, media, social agencies, clubs and associations, businesses, volunteer organizations, foundations and funding sources, government, and especially institutes dealing with aging and gerontology) to pursue a broad range of programs. These programs can provide learning in critical areas, as follows: basic literacy, psychology and social living, finance and employment planning, philosophy and spirituality, family values, intercultural relations, drug and alcohol abuse, mental health, child-rearing, medical care and health, death and dying, cultural arts and personal creativity, career skill upgrades, time management, and social consciousness, etc.

a. Serve as *honest* role models for children and adults by questioning the "ignorance" of our "proselytizations of truth," which are touted as wisdom or the "voice of experience." Feel unafraid to engage with others (including young minds) in exploring alternate views of goodness, value, success, competence, justice, and other "foundation principles" we utilize in relating to others, and our "selves." In fact, the current worldwide paradigm shift projects that every culture will be forced to understand beliefs and values of *all* peoples in a newly *synergistic* global environment.

b. View adult life similarly to childhood, with its unique crises and stages of "developmental challenge." These demarcations constitute points at which "explanations of reality" have exhausted their utility (completion of career "ladder," empty-nest syndrome, economic or personal loss). Also note that major "gaps" in "rationalization" present opportunities to "expand awareness" beyond our limited scope of "understanding." New visions are required relative to poverty and suffering in a Christian world, unexplainable tragic or miraculous happenings in our lives, out-of-body experiences, special dreams or sensory awarenesses, etc. We may anticipate "junctures in ideologic continuity" in adult futures, and educationally prepare, to diminish unnecessary emotional suffering, and to accentuate pleasure from intellectual and spiritual growth.

c. Participate (as worker, organizer, funder) in community volunteer work, public projects, or private organizational outreach efforts (University Continuing Education programs, business training opportunities, etc.), to encourage societal involvement in educating everyone to the highest degree possible. Remember that an "educated" community sociologically represents an environment with (1) greater productivity and economic well-being, (2) less crime and violent approaches to problem-solving, (3) control of population densities which overburden ecologic aesthetics and economic sustenance ratios, (4) higher employment salaries generally, (5) decreased taxation burdens for welfare programs, (6) enhanced cultural opportunities, and (7) greater "participative democratic" philosophies and governmental activities to utilize everyone's creative ideas/talents.

Principle #6: Develop an interest for involvement in the assessment, creation and evaluation of formal educational curricula from preschool through university doctoral training. The world's view and approach to knowing, understanding, and interacting with "us," is "programmed." Appreciate that "mind-sets" represent value principles, problem-solution formulas, life "agenda" perspectives, and beliefs about "responsibility," in the minds (and "hearts") of students at all levels. Consider that the only "true" legacy of the social, psychological, and spiritual components of our "relevancy," exists within thoughts and mental energies that evolve in the educational experiences of youth. Unfortunately, industrial urban society has "exploded" to the extent that socialization (education for living) has been "relegated" to formal institutions of learning. Therefore, parents or concerned adults must share powers of influence upon young people, with curriculum "designers and implementers." Although well-meaning, these individuals make unilateral decisions about "what" and "how" to teach, and have great autonomy, in choosing what children will "know" about realities of "this" or "other" life domains. Curriculum remains stable for multiple generations, so innovations in thinking and sharing knowledge experience "culture-lag," when new perceptions are needed. Some subdimensions of the nature of school curricula, therefore, are as follows:

a. "Facts" which are taught should be nestled evaluatively within a framework of "human motivations" and cultural "exigencies" which produce a "temporary" or "permanent" truth. Students should explore opposing or alternate ideas to understand the subjective and objective processes of cognitive decision-making which "evolve" in society.

b. Children at earliest possible ages should be exposed to philosophic, spiritual, religious, psychologic and sociologic "sciences," as *foundations* upon which "facts" have meaning, and life has "relevancy."

c. Education should include content on psycho- and socio-"pathologies." These range from "deviant" reactions in all of us to developmental conflicts and situational crises, to equally "entrapping" social "conformity" and "mindless" dependency on *cultural* definitions.

d. Students must be "empowered" by the influential teacher-student relationship to develop sensible, responsible, socially-conscious, but *independent* self-governance and decisioning capabilities. This helps avoid permanent "recapitulation" of parent-dominated ideations, and enables evolving minds to create "contemporary realities" which are functional and humane for each cohort's "eco-phenomenal" environment. It also avoids regression to antiquated truths which, may never be validated, even if longitudinal persistence ignores "exception."

e. Education must understand the difference between listening/observing/attending/perceiving/accepting, etc. as the *only* "communicational" (data input) mechanisms for growing. We should also skeptically view presumed virtues of talking/describing/analyzing/self-confirming, etc. as exemplars of "being educated." We learn very little communicating what we "already know," although culture offers reward for "competency demonstrations." If oversubscribed, these give the illusion that we continue to learn, rather than simply re-create "memorized" or "understood" learning from the past.

f. Children must learn skills for "living," which are usually ignored by "scientific" curricula. Theoretical concepts "refer to," but "are not" direct experiences of some dimensions of life which children should know ("be"). This range of topics includes child birth and rearing, sexuality, developing or terminating relationships, preparing for death, building family or intimate living environments, sharing and accepting responsibility, having and using feelings, health care and nutrition, using community resources, planning futures, understanding history, employment preparation, proper uses of drugs (including alcohol and other sensory-influencing substances), understanding government, learning as a lifelong pursuit, handling illness, dealing with loss, utilizing recreation, etc.

g. Creativity, innovativeness, skill-development, self-enhancement, sensuality, energy utilization, perceptual acuity, and cognitive stimulation—should be theoretically explored and experientially practiced. This enables young persons to develop awareness of their "specialness." Learners should maximize talents for personal satisfaction, and "integrate" capabilities between people, to improve collective adaptation and community "synergy" for the welfare of all. This includes appreciation of "causes" of limitations in others, "costs" of human deprivations and opportunity abridgements, and "responsibilities" for human rights advocacy.

Chapter IV

PEACE AND INTERNATIONAL CONFLICT

The evolution of intercultural "critical mass" explosive energy, produces lethal aggressive attacks and "defensive" retaliations with weapons of war. Ideologically, this reflects accumulations of insular, deductive, and antecedent "conclusion formulation" which assumes the following: (1) reductions of freedom of "choice," (2) mandated self-protections, (3) abrogations of ideologic eminence, (4) maximization of uncontrollable anxiety, and (5) compulsive initiations of "power-obtaining" military functions. These "truths of conflict" appear as confusing, frightening and overwhelming scenarios of "mega-proportions," which cause us to disparagingly resolve to let someone else "figure it out." Although most will never become "principal actors" in this life and death drama, a responsible adult should, at least, analyze the "process" of international alienation. Each of us *may* discover opportunities to become involved in early stages of the more manageable snowballing "cultural alienational phenomena." Awareness insures that individual thoughts and behaviors are *not* "pathogenetic" auto-intoxications which contribute to pervasive atrophy of "sound reasoning," that results in the insanity of human destruction of humanity. The following, therefore, is a brief overview of *necessary* and *sufficient* conditions, providing predisposing "atmospheres," where national aggression emerges as a "solution" to predefined "problems."

Ideology and "Belief" Systems

The basic predisposing factor to international alienation, polarized political "positioning," military defensive "gridlock" systems, and economic-political zero sum competition—is the fundamental fact that people *"think."* Additionally, they think that *what* they think is the "truth." All of us are plagued with child-socialized values. These result in lifetime quests to undo the entrapment of *vulnerable dependency* and its associated behavioral constrictions on each self's autonomous thought, feeling, and experience. We possess a miraculous cognitive computer which symbolizes "material" and "imaginary" reality through the neurobiologic "electrification" of concepts. These representations are "reified" by thinkers as actual "domains of essence" which elucidate and validate, in our minds, various forms of "permanency." We assume that "solid" values can be utilized as evaluative criteria to differentiate quality—which is a second primordial quest of humankind—the search for *relevancy.*

As we "think," therefore, we construct mental worlds which "seem" to extend into infinite wide-open spaces. Herein, we create images of ultimate "significances" or global attributes of value. We believe, commensurately, that these values are obtainable and reinforcing "sheathes of efficaciousness" which can be applied to various actions or conditions of the body or spiritual soul. We believe that value, idea, motivation, and action are equally interchangeable and rationally predictable. Since we "take on" hierarchical characteristics of "beings" with discriminative assets of "quality" ("difference" rather than "better/worseness"), we fabricate contingencies and interactional categories of behavior in the "here and now." When occurring, these references transport us automatically into a more energized and intensified "there and then." We index mundane behavior relative to a better place of autonomy, justice, and celebration of a purer and more regal "self." By ignoring contemporary behavioral limitations, we mentally undertake any "journeys" we desire, to transcend the natural dimensions of human vulnerability. These, as you recall, are initially experienced with "permanent unconscious potency" in early childhood. In mental "chess games," we "become more" than we think we are, or more than we think other people think we are, and symbolically escape limitations of biologic life. We think we need to accomplish this because our indefatigably searching minds learn that "naturalness" is a "negative," leading ultimately to death and extreme nothingness. We free ourselves from negativity of dependency on early childhood parental control and domination, of the free spirit of life energy. In dealing with fears of vulnerability, we become involved in social relationships with parents, peers, and other adults later on. As these networks become "life forms" themselves, we further escape as the relevant "self" is affirmed "knowably" by pragmatically and esoterically discriminating one "self" from other "selves." We view this strategy as a power differential in the relationships we have with parents who are different and powerful "selves" that are *not* our "selves." Imagined "formulas of value" imply a *greater degree of relevance* of the individual self, relative to its own nature. This idea is externalized to reduce anxiety and fear when we realize we cannot *really* transcend ourselves. We can however, wage a battle within our own minds, that is transported symbolically outside our selves to relatively safer relationships with others. We unconsciously believe that others (e.g., "foreigners"), *have* to be different but "less than" us.

Dependency

Another childhood-endemic process as a necessary, but not yet sufficient, ingredient for anti-"thetical" international "postures" and "procedures," is "birth-traumatic" and infantile fear. "Being born" is compounded by extensive dependency on authority figures and belief systems/role structures. Natural childhood trepidation is cumulatively socialized into the *perceived "need"* for superordinate norms and values to dictate the "correct" ways of living (transcending feared futility of "animal-evolved" life). Associated *systems of organization* (culture) insure predictable relations between people who as children, and as adults, compete for scarce resources of parental nurturance and physical subsistence. "Structures" serve various authority functions to dominate the fearful child in us, who does not *really* want responsibility for its own survival and "relevancy." Social structures ordain ritualized behaviors which (1) occupy time, (2) fill space, (3) provide stimulation, (4) supply symbolized "scapegoats" for anger at human vulnerability and precarious/uncertain existence, and (5) function as an excuse for personal irresponsibility which prevents failure of the self in *direct* interaction with only itself, or with the universal environment.

What happens sequentially involves several integrated *functions of survival:*

1. *Dependency* on the presumed passive and naturally "sensitive" *environment* (resources must be discovered, extracted, transformed, transported, stored, marketed, disposed) causes systems of production. We "do the work" of feeding and sheltering humankind, based on physical need to survive, and psychological fear of pain, starvation, or death.

2. Psychologic *dependency* on *parents* signifies human vulnerability, and needs for emotional sustenance from a presumed limited (due to parental psycho-biologic limitations) "reservoir" of comforting "commodities." This attitude reinforces "productivity," to achieve personal security.

3. *Dependency* on *others* ensues *initially,* for physical survival as resources are difficult to modify for human use, or become scarce with consumption. *Secondarily,* dependence continues with parental substitutes, when needs for autonomy (the mind's escape from debilitating dependency into a world of anticipated freedom) push us to form "adult" relationships to supply psycho-emotional sustenance.

4. *Dependency* on *organizational systems* emerges (business, finance, government) to (a) provide collective energy to overcome production obstacles through integration of skills to produce "profit" (food, money, leisure time) and (b) "control" individual strivings to insure survival. This is "necessary"

because we retain infantile recollections (unconscious fears) of all-consuming animal instincts for survival (this includes "devouring our own" or the *environment* if hunger plus fear reach critical levels relative to environmental-"yield" ratios). These inclinations were "inherited" in competitive relationships with siblings or peers seeking "fair shares" of attention and emotional "caring" from adults (presumed repositories of emotional profit). We learned to compete (earn, justify, elicit, access, etc.) for needed "units of nurturance" from parents, who utilize systems of emotional reinforcement or withdrawal to induce behavioral and attitudinal conformity among children. Parents support their own needs for relevance through continuation of the self within other selves which are "reproduced."

5. *Dependency* on *ideology*, "progresses," which is the basic foundation of "theory" to accomplish these tasks:

   a. explain the rationale for instinctual survival behaviors among "advanced" anthropo-social organisms; whose minds note that materialistic survival makes little sense from holistic standpoints (why gain in order to lose, why live for pleasure when nonliving does not necessarily represent pain, etc.);

   b. provide checks and balances on "animal instincts" which become destructive as perceived or real need-deprivation rises;

   c. elevate irrelevant, or nonexistent life "beyond" its physical limitations into a "zone of comprehensive value," which transforms what "is" or "is not" into what might be "better" or *less* "is"; and finally,

   d. cause dependency on ideology to provide a rationale for "differentiation," which is the way things "are" when children perceive themselves as "not" their parents and, therefore, need autonomy to elevate the self from irrelevancy; yet interaction with other selves causes fear, because *they* may (1) achieve greater relevancy, or (2) cause us to perceive lesser degrees of self-competence.

Competition

A third component in the "stew" of developmental international conflict that results in a "schizo-paradoxical" win-lose "stalemate" is *competition:*

1. Competition develops *intrapsychically* from reward-punishment child-rearing techniques. Assets or deficits of material necessities (e.g., food, clothing)

are "extrapolated" as parallel attributes (amounts intervally or ordinally added/subtracted to assumed potential zero [0] quantities) of emotional or spiritual "residuals" within the "corporealized" self or system of interacting "selves." Attributes, are *earned* through attitudinal or behavioral competition between child and parent, or internally between "good and bad" aspects of the child's "characteristics."

2. Competition develops *socially*, as multiplying numbers of "needy subsisters" place demands on diminishing natural, or limited family/community emotional resources, wherein:

   a. inherent or learned fears of extinction produce escalating efforts to obtain and stockpile "critical commodities";

   b. competition is culturally mediated, to avoid violence and obliteration of resource reserves and natural replenishment systems;

   c. culture authorizes economic token systems (money) which are (1) "illusions of resources" that are acquired, saved, or spent at moderate and incrementally staggered rates, to insure need-meeting without destroying "foundation" resources, (2) power-wielding symbols of the "objectified" personality ("my" money, "our" property)—the above weapon-like extensions of the aggressive "animalistic organism" sustain competitive desires while remaining at a distance from actual vulnerable selves which:

      (1) realize the irrationality of the "game" and don't want its various "moves" close enough to have to assume responsibility (or irresponsibility),

      (2) need a complex system of ritualized exchange to "fill in the gaps" between earned stages of competitive achievement, and,

      (3) require some form of winning/reciprocally not losing, to validate perceptions of competition in unconscious, and conscious, identity.

When competition expands into multinational market economics and "high finance," the "personality-vulnerability" scenario is simply *expanded* to include more participants and a wider array of products. Larger amounts of capital (perceived emotional asset or deficit) are manipulated to accomplish the following:

1. Capital reduces competitive options and power of others. Minimal wages transferred between alternating groups of "needy" earners, "lock" threatening populations into stable subsidiary work roles. Workers compete for wages that are (a) high enough to "save" them from starvation, (b) high enough to purchase (control) their loyalty to consistent production (which reduces everyone's fear), (c) low enough to prevent substantial property ownership, or self-improvement to catapult larger numbers of people into scarce managerial roles of powerful class-elites.

2. Capital secures mass quantities of raw materials or resource "energies" (to do work to change other resources) to provide "nationalized security" (symbolized protection of the child within). Countries control "needs" of other nations by selling at a profit, buying less in return than is sold, but buying enough to insure control of export business. They use sale profits to increase military strength and develop more resources.

3. Capital creates and maintains complex systems of banking for borrowing and lending. These (a) lead to interdependent "stagnatizing" of undetermined capacities of aggression (need-satisfaction with diminishing resources, wherein aggression is a negative correlation of diminishing assets *and* diminishing resources which precipitate accumulations of internal pressure and fear), which are "litigated" by credit agreements. Banking also (b) controls predictable markets which need money to initiate resource conversion and production, to create resources of capital to buy profit-generating products from the "prime lender." The borrower is assured of being competitively controlled by the lender because of interest payments "mandated" on the original production-initiation loan.

In these combined aspects of competition, original fears and destructive perceptions of reality are exchanged for "safer" and more comprehensively time/attention consuming "operations." These operations become examples of *human alienation* from the intrinsic "self" initially, and from other "selves" which are assumed to possess motivation to deprive the original perceiving self of its relevant "selfhood." The perceiving mind "assumes" the ego system is the rational structure to evolve from basic organic biology. But, this system is compared presumptively to a "negative non-self," so that competition for material and spiritual commodities must essentially be one of the following options:

1. Competition is natural genetic biochemistry instinctively perpetuating its own existence as programmed naturally.

2. Competition is advanced animal-genetic-plus-socially-learned survival technique, including complex abstraction of relationships between other "needy organisms."

3. Competition is purely intrapsychic sensory-based and rational fear of pain. It has a superimposed cognitive illusion (the mind insanely going beyond itself) of loss of relevancy, expanded into an interpersonal network of ritualized behaviors. Animalistic instincts are boosted with emotional implications, or are only meaningful relative to created delusions of significance.

Codification

One reason for conflicts of international magnitude, with threats of military and econo-political retaliation, is because there *are* norms, rules, treaties, laws, and configurations of agreements. "Codes" of conduct and attitude, in fact, directly prohibit violent conflict, or conversely encourage maintenance of positive relationships ("Let's make a deal" with cultural exchange, business agreements, trade stipulations, diplomatic opportunities, philosophical compendia, etc.). Sadly, the *process* of "formalizing" human relationships has never worked definitively in marriage, work contracts, consumer guarantees, international politics, etc., as a fundamental solution to chronic inter-human alienation (under ideal circumstances it provides a "band-aid" temporary "delaying action"):

1. Rules or laws are enforced by "superior powers" *to* inferior powers, just as children experience parental "dictates." The exploratory human mind (spirit), seeking "salvation" of the autonomous "self" and true independence, ultimately *rejects* the *rules,* and *resents* the *rule-maker* in order to experience freedom.

2. Rules are compulsive ritualized defenses which signify automatic vulnerability of the co-adherents. They provide immediate pseudo-functional respite from fears of "nothingness," and the irrelevancy of non-being. These fears emerge as gaps in comprehensive or specific explanations of reality when the laws are pragmatically or logically extended to their full, but always limited, extent. This is especially true where exceptions to policy represent human characteristics or ideologic principles which are "illogical."

3. Rules are challenges to creative minds, to discover innovative nuances or "detoured excursions" into deviant waters (which are "assumed" removals of imprisoning controls). Human mental capability, plus socially sanctioned

productivity orientations, *routinely* produce *variations* on common themes, thus rendering static agreements as cumulatively irrelevant, especially as rules enforce compliance to other rules.

4. Rules or agreements are focal stimuli that detract "productive" attention from concerns of common humanity, and, as noted in committee meetings, embroil participants in "micro-insani-cratic minutiae." This "distraction" is an authoritarian mechanism to control disruptive innovations, and allows conspiratorial collective abdications of responsibility when the "authority of law" reigns or inhibits.

5. Rules, by their very existence, suggest negative aspects of human differentiation (Iraqi's must be strange because we have codes to translate meanings and to "force similarities"). They lack flexibility as human need, awareness, or developmental conditions change ("I agreed to marry you and remain faithful forever when we were 21 years old; but at age 35, you and I are different, but still bound by the earlier mandate which did not change with our development"). Also, rules prevent meaningful associations based on emotional similarity or interdependent need-meeting, because the law ineffectively defines these "essences of self" for us.

Poverty and Class Distinctions

The previous four necessary, but not sufficient conditions, contribute greatly to the "illogically deduced rationale" for armed conflict as a solution to human survival and significance "dilemmas." The mind's struggle (individual and collective) to interface with, and "take charge" of, its ingenerate vulnerability and mortality, is partly a physical "compatibility" correlation. Adaptation involves planning and executing need-meeting behaviors relative to environmental attributes which satisfy these strivings. Life is also, however, a complex "cognitive game" composed of the following elements:

1. The mind plays the game of *"transcendence."*

2. The mind arranges super-valuational *intensification* of emotions. This is probably projected simulation of neuro-sensory stimulation which, in childhood, signaled danger, but in adulthood is converted and redefined as "controllable ecstasy" of self-relevance.

3. The mind arranges ideas in *hierarchical structuring* of desired conditions, of being-in-progression toward greater "ultimacy."

4. The mind thinks in formulas of "quali-predictable" *differentiation* of the self *from* "nothingness," *from* external material reality, and *from* other "beings" who may be sources of food within the "animal kingdom" (can I eat me or things like me). In this context, others are viewed as inferior (potentially superior) to generate motivation and a rationale for competition for food-shelter-rest, etc. The mind, evolutionarity, develops culturally representational referents, as abstract ideas. It searches restlessness to "elaborate" on each of its concept-creations. Differentiation must, of course, occur predominantly at higher levels of abstraction because of gross similarities of human physiology, and the reproductive need of highly integrated inter-gender "oneness." This paradox is mitigated and diametrically polarized when "men's minds" are controlled by their maternal creator's will, and by the "irrational" necessity of catapulting oneself away from the nest in order to hunt and gather food. Women can't do this totally while bearing children, and need the "insurance" of younger males to handle subsistence demands while reproduction cycles are occurring (the she-primate differentiates from mother to connect with differentiated men).

There is a problem, however, with these psychodynamic creations of ultimate or semi-ultimate domains of relevancy, and syllogistic explanation of the "unexplainable." There is no linear reasoning that leads from "mental manipulation of reality" to handle fear, dependency, differentiation, etc.—to concomitant display of military aggression and critical "massing" of frustrated energy which produces war. The existence of *poverty,* or near poverty conditions, in Third World or industrial nations therefore, represents "incubational fertilizer." From this stimulus, two other *necessary* conditions grow for the emergence of prewar "national mentalities" and development of military-industrial systems. These compete with, and "check" (chess analogy) each other in the "acting out" of principles related to "alleged" abrogations of human dignity, civil rights, international protocol, economic detente, etc.:

1. The first condition occurs in *preindustrial "Third World" countries.* Massive subhuman deprivation, with limited natural resource reserves, produces a "ripe environment" for emergence of pathologic, paranoid, sociopathic charismatic leaders (plus the less militarily powerful, healthier spiritual leader, e.g., Ghandi, Buddha, Christ, etc.). The despot accents instability and precipitates conflict with "richer" countries.

2. The second condition develops in *socioeconomically more stable environments* which, nevertheless, have large welfare obligations, plus increasing economic demands (greed) of emerging *middle-class* workers. In this context, two confluential ideologic gaps energize each other. The poor seek "victory of self" via unavailable economic means, and the middle class

realizes that money doesn't buy the complete victory of the self. This creates, not a unitary charismatic despot, but a "nationalism" of progressive ideologic searching which results in (a) arrogant "evangelism" of "insufficient pagan peoples," (b) exploratory pressures to conquer new worlds by the middle classes with time—but decreasing meaning of life—on their hands, (c) domination of unproductive cultures, to open labor and consumer markets to compensate for unreasonable wage demands on the home front, (d) defensive militarism to protect against retaliation by countries which have been exploited for material gains.

Each of the above conditions will be elaborated below:

a. *Third World Countries:* In these cases, a preponderant middle class is absent. There is limited consumer buying power, minimal bureaucratic organization of society, and insufficient intellectual, spiritual, and philosophical symbolic life agendas to "stabilize" the social order. There is no mediation between minority elite and majority poor classes. Herein, charismatic military leaders find a foothold among large numbers of unemployed young men (women of this age have satisfied stability and transcension "needs" by having babies and maintaining "households") needing "outlets" for "deprivation-based," "productivity-sterile," and physiologically ripening energies. These deficits are used by despots to control people and resources, and coerce an extravagant lifestyle from primary industries and military acquisitions which emerge. The sociopathic or paranoid autocrat (1) utilizes spiritual or emotional principles of human "idealism" to placate and romanticize the suffering of poverty, (2) focuses resentful attention on the imperialistic capitalism of "Westernized philosophy," which they discourage because it replaces monarchy, and (3) maintains economic subsistence through [a] liaisons with other Third World cultures who consolidate to perpetuate criminal and military resource acquisitions, [b] backdoor support from major industrial powers to conduct guerrilla warfare against competitors' means of production or distribution, [c] limited allowance of industrial development which provides income from percentage export duties and purchase of property, although never becomes entrenched enough to threaten displacement of the ruling faction, and [d] terrorist "blackmail" in the form of "free" social development monies, bank loans (which are never repaid), or foreign diplomatic and humanitarian "restabilization aid" from which the sovereign ruler siphons a large profit.

World peace, of course, is threatened, because superpower industries (and their bureaucratic governmental "errand boys/girls") have vested interest in sustained poverty, to maintain a plethora of inexpensive labor for various aspects of product development. They do not *really* want stability, in the short run, without substantial economic control of property, natural resources, military "vantage points" and trade routes/locations (stability means equal competition for resources, labor, market shares, political power, etc.). There is advantage in the poverty-based instability and military volatility of Third World "strike forces" who can be used and blamed for aggression against economic and political enemies. This is accomplished without diplomatic embarrassment to the major industrial powers, who plan and use these "irrational" acts for strategic economic/political advantage. Treaties or symbolic agreements with "unstable leadership groups" are, of course, ineffectual because (1) fertile conditions of gross human suffering recurrently produce new "tough guys" who promise sufferers a "way out" against imperialist domination on the road to their true "Godhead," (2) the desperate conditions are necessary for acquisition of cheap property, and profit-motivated control of disorganized and needy labor, and (3) the focal point of "human suffering" easily becomes the scape-goat or sacrificial arena within which economic battles are renamed "philosophical" wars of ideology. This gives a *unification theme* to impressionable and frustrated forces of terrorism utilized by the autocrat, and perpetuates cultural disorganization because disparate "philosophers" never talk the same language. Agreement and issuing democracy will never threaten the despot's potential to "slip through the gaps" and seize control.

b. *Stable industrial "powers":* In these societies, poverty also plays an important role in the war-peace dilemma. This is not a direct source of militaristic person-power or a "vulnerable corridor" through which the autocratic ruler (or external industrial production organization) rushes to seize power. It is rather, an insidious, subtle phenomenon against which business and government must react to justify their own existence, but also their illogical and irrelevant procedures for maintaining existence. Factors which combine to produce military complexes, supported by nationalistic philosophies are as follows:

(1) Poverty looms as a gross empirical *"expletive"* of psychosocial *failure,* which serves as a stimulus for bureaucratic support of a middle class. The "middle" will not challenge corporate production ownership, but remains a stable "consumer audience," trapped in a predictable and conservative social role. Prospective incumbents of the middle class feel incorrectly (but understandably, due to dependency, fear and vulnerability) that they have

been competitive with the poor and one another to achieve "success." Such efforts are stimulated by (a) a superimpositional "ethic" of capitalistic-based productivity, Judeo-Christian spiritual achievement, (b) compulsive and defensive management of "ideation," (c) sublimation of aggressive/sexual energy, (d) behavioral reward contingencies (recapitulation of childhood vulnerability) and "need" for excitation and stimulation—without poverty, there is nothing visible to fear ("Hell" is too obscure a concept for money to integrate).

(2) The ever-present potential to "lazily earn" poverty, and mandates for the poor to justify suffering in the lands of milk, honey and BMW's, combine to produce "security nets" (psychic insurance policies) of "human ideology." Middle classes use these to compensate for awareness (guilt) of discrepancies between "self and suffering other." Poor people also "employ" these nets to rise above pain (they don't have "real" employment). In both cases of *"functional"* belief, the part that contributes most to non-peace is ideology, as a set of *"qualitative differentiations"* of "essences" which necessarily *must* separate peoples' "souls" from one another.

(3) Continual *contradictions* of ideology, as noted in representational materialistic examples (some "good" people are poor and some "bad" people are rich), means that culture needs a system to maintain the "faith." This system of belief produces *religious* rituals, managers of rituals, and *institutions* to manage the managers and their constituents. This does not void the possibility that religion and spiritual roles also deduce from divine direction, providence or inspiration. In fact, spirituality may be socially "functional" to the exclusion of, or in addition to, "pure" religious missions. This process, however, of consolidating and proselytizing about ideologic beliefs, necessarily differentiates the "haves" from the "have nots." Vast discriminations of human and spiritual conditions of being, grace, quality, purity, etc. naturally emerge. This is alienation from one vantage point, and also is related to social hierarchies. Religious doctrines can only be "marketed" within the structures of economically successful institutions, whose constituents represent large portions of poor people whose combined meager income supports a religion (as well as government) and helps keep the poor, poor.

(4) The need to survive, and desire to maintain large industrial city populations, means that production within complex societies necessitates perpetuation of large numbers of "cheap" laborers. This insures competition for jobs and higher production profit margins. Cheap labor maintains "relatively" low inflationary ceilings on wages, which always go up with costs, because resources necessarily diminish for lengthy periods of time between world revolutions. This *enables warlike behaviors* from civilized industrial and complex mega-cultures: (a) large numbers of *poor,* although "necessary" for business, *drain social bank accounts* with welfare costs, which periodically means that military-related economic surges are necessary to produce greater work effort among frightened and patriotic employees to enhance productivity; (b) recurrent trends in conservative economic spending among middle classes, who fear poverty and respond to increasing product costs, necessitates military intervention "overseas" to seek control of "free resources" to [1] destroy local production to stimulate import needs, [2] precipitate military defensive preparations which means massive increments in "back-door" or "third party retail" sales of military paraphernalia, produced by the "perpetrating power," and [3] reap financial benefits during reconstruction phases of the "loser's" history (e.g., bank loans, construction and engineering services, materials, advisors, tourism, etc.); (c) poor people who lack economic or political "buffering" against governmental power [1] can easily be "sacrificed" in battle to "justify" cultured society's aggressive, profit-motivated militarism, [2] have high levels of idealism which produces heroic military service, [3] lack education to understand the "real" reasons for war, and [4] serve as ideologic reference points for patriotic efforts to "help" disadvantaged populations in "savage" countries; (d) increasing frustration and potential revolution of "underclasses" can be subverted, and attention shifted, by engaging externally focused aggressions against outside (rather than internal) enemies, which produces national unification, and provides an outlet for aggressions which might otherwise disrupt economic and sociopolitical stability; (e) the perpetual presence of the "lowest echelons" of social orders and the "bankrupt essence" of hopeful humanity unconsciously, and directly, [1] reminds middle classes of the irrelevance of the "spiritually" symbolic material artifacts which they accumulate for "self-actualization," so that [2] recurrent shifts in consumer "fetishes" (keep searching for the "truth") creates instability within the marketplace, compensated for by the

poor who purchase "leftovers" to avoid loss to production and retail; their presence also [3] provides stability among middle-class consumers and military and military support personnel who occupy institutional jobs of a conservative nature to "hold poor classes in their place." The periodic "clash of swords" around the world reminds people of the dangers of "liberalism" and revolution, and conversely supports conservation and consequent market stability.

(5) The last "function" of poverty, relative to war potential, concerns natural "parental" needs of "superior" classes to *take care of* vulnerable children. This unfortunately, does not "materialize," so that residues of collective guilt can be expiated with high visibility international "thrusts of rehabilitative justice and moral retribution" to defend "underdogs" and "free peoples" everywhere.

Progressive Idealism

Another precursor of regional or national aggressions relates physically to the stimulus-seeking/needing nature and "instinctual" energy of the human sensory system. This system is "expanded" throughout maturation into socially sanctioned concepts of progression, achievement, developmental movement, acquisition, etc. Cumulative "attainment" of various levels of stimulation results in "tolerance conditions" where larger doses are needed to produce desirable effects. Also, the "cognitive attachment" of conceptual symbols to neurophysical chemical and cellular predispositions, insures *inability* of "conceptualized statures" to ever satisfy physical needs. This occurs because they are inherently *incomparable domains* of life or "animation process," and because concepts are open-ended (no inherent substance—only materially "representational" substance). Therefore, they never provide "boundaried containers of representational life," and there is simultaneously "no path, and no end to the path" of life's journey. Simultaneous experiences of "particularism" and "universalism" create frustration, and "frontiers" of an ultimate and "external" nature become necessary:

1. "Ultimacy" *prevents insanity* as the system (or person) contemplates "infinite" dimensions of itself with a "finite" instrument (cerebral cortex), and perceives limitations of human vulnerability with a seemingly unboundaried mind (soul, spirit, heart, consciousness).

2. "Ultimacy" *demonstrates "progress"* when material or philosophical answers reach "generational dead ends." New horizons of domination of natural or

human resistance (not the self, however, because dreams of immortality are destroyed—but foreign "selves" can be conquered) can be "tested."

3. "Ultimacies" *obtain new perspectives* by force, so the conqueror is obliged to appreciate the views of the victim who must be rebuilt emotionally and culturally. The dominating society does not admit that its own values have become useless, irrelevant, ludicrous, frightening, insane, nonexistent, etc.

4. "Ultimacies" *force genetic interaction* to overcome "inherent and learned" boredom of "similitude," which blocks the "stimulus hunger" of perceptual and social selves. Cultural stability produces conservative reproduction of people and artifacts which are *very much like* their creators. As this happens, we desperately "break out" of the eco-consonant environment (psychic vacation) and force ourselves to "be something different." Forceful military and political action is a sufficiently powerful thrust to alter entrenched ways of life, which, without change, ultimately destroys itself. Conservative motives, however, demand that the culture or individually trapped person take drastic steps to handle the dissonance that accompanies change (e.g., it took powerful self-action to propel me personally from a stable and lengthy marriage when I needed change but was afraid to change—I "fought" my way out—just like "war").

Bureaucracy

The final "necessary" condition for international tension, where solutions are obscured or defeated, is the "apparently functional," but exaggerated, role of governmental theory, organization, and operation. These systems are seen within complex industrial cultures but also on a smaller scale in "less developed" preindustrial societies. The social order and daily operating activities of "growing" cultures must be regulated. This is necessary even though standardization occurs as a "holding device" "within" and "between" conflictual intra-societal subgroups or socioeconomic classes. Standardization is expected to accomplish the following: (1) support autonomous variations and progressions of industrial (or now techno-industrial-service) production, while reducing instability in other arenas, (2) insure consistent distribution of goods and services, to meet demands that middle-class labor makes of the poor (insure supply of low wage competitors, fill unattractive and mundane jobs, prevent guilt relative to massive "genocidal extinction") and the demands of the rich who own means of production and prime property (3) uphold cultural norms through development, storage and dissemination of "codes of value":

1. "Ethical codes" maintain (a) standards and practices for discouragement or punishment of deviance, (b) "glorification" of social rituals to occupy the attention of dormant or frustrated psycho-emotional "systems," and (c) conservatism to dispel "collectively conscious" fears of the "unknown." They concurrently allow "controlled" excursions into the "insane" world of unrestrained physiology, free thought, or comprehensive passivity (roller coasters, scary movies, massive group activities, vacation resorts, sexual stimulation, etc.).

2. Cultural standards enhance the availability of ideologic transcendental advanced levels of consciousness and being, through arts and recreation for the middle and upper classes. "Going Beyond" occurs through unconscious and vicarious allowance of drug, alcohol, violence, and sexuality experiences for the under and over classes. Both processes, allow us to purchase different qualities of the commodity ("vehicle" to transcend the self) at different prices.

Although bureaucracy, per se, is not "patho-indicative" of interpersonal relationship dysfunction, the *way* it operates, and its inherent discouragement of deviant confrontations of its process, perpetuates "typical government." The peace-related deficits of bureaucracy are these:

1. *Stereotypes:* Bureaucracies standardize operations by maintaining consistent definitions of people and situations, to maintain intra-class "equality" and streamline activities. Unfortunately, concepts of unique individuality, which integrate universal humanity, are lost. Stereotyping demands conservatism, which demands cumbersome "checks and balances" in the system, which produces crippling fears of autonomous decision-making ("rubber stamp" and "carbon copy" syndromes develop).

2. *Retardation:* Bureaucracies move slow in an indirect effort to control random variation and crises in the culture, and to idealistically allow "competent" deductive-inductive rational decisioning. This slowness sacrifices sensitivity and effective responsiveness to human needs, resulting in accumulations of skepticism and resentment that are expressed internationally in aggressions against "structures" of government.

3. *Resistance:* Bureaucracies maintain rigid boundaries around themselves to preserve the "myth" of functional effectiveness, and insulate against destructive autonomous thinking and behaving. Standard operating procedures and rigid rules of inclusion or exclusion, result in mutual checkmate conditions when the bureaucracy of one country "deals with" its foreign counterpart.

4. *Paranoia:* Bureaucracies, and those within them, view "outsiders" as "enemies," because human needs vary beyond capacities of organizational structures. Individuality must be "negated" or "negativized" to justify the impersonality of organizational structures, which are alleged to "represent" people. Ultimately, efforts to stimulate bureaucratic responsiveness are interpreted as "offensive" intrusions which must be defended against.

5. *Role Decay:* Monotonous repetition of bureaucratic jobs which mitigate creativity and autonomy of employees, results in "burned-out" and bored "clerks" whose life excitements are "estranged" from professional work roles. Conservatism further encourages "tenuring" of "automatons" who are incompetent enough to maintain equilibrium and absence of crisis-producing thought and action. Bureaucratic "gatekeepers" from different countries, who ceased caring about themselves or other people, produce alienational communication channels that push compassion farther into the background.

6. *Irresponsibility:* The size and complication of bureaucratic structures allow frightened inhabitants to recapture comfortable dependency roles with controlling parental figures (authorities). Personal "failure" is never realized (bureaucracies are existential insurance policies) since the organization is too big to influence, and too powerful to control—we "assume" that "safe" is "better" than "sorry."

7. *Standardized Procedure:* The intent of bureaucracy to control the variability of phenomena which illustrate "anomalies" in "universal life theory," means that counteroffensive sequences of protectionism are pre-programmed among staff, to reduce fear of organizational destruction (structural, functional, phenomenologic "irrelevance"). The consequent results (the movie *Fail Safe*) are that "robots" are conditioned to follow orders, and do so religiously to avoid ostracism for deviance—even if rationality or humane sanity is the "cause."

8. *Sadism:* Instinctual survival mechanisms in "computers" of primates, stimulate destructive attack on natural prey to survive and handle fears of reciprocal destruction. Fight or flight responses are "normal," to satisfy the most basic human subsistence needs, and are sublimated within various aspects of power-wielding bureaucratic assaults on individual social or cultural victims. There is simultaneous abdication of responsibility for either animal anthropomorphic heritage, or conflictual psychic defensive postures of human aggression.

9. *Collusion:* "Unhuman" economic materialsm, and dependency on powerful systems of industrial production controlled by an "entrepreneurial elite," suggests complicity between such elites and "autonomy-seeking" individuals and "ideology-aspiring" collectivities. We obscure "realities" of human life, through systems of living which maintain policies of human "altruism," but also "labyrinths" of operations, so that industry and business can "slip through the cracks" and receive support and allegiance. Conglomerates avoid direct detection by groups of citizens large enough to collectively support fairness and equalitarian balance. Since bureaucracy and its political functionaries support self-serving (but also community serving) profit-seeking business without community awareness of what is really happening, a giant Wizard of Oz syndrome exists.

10. *Consumerism:* Finally, bureaucracy maintains "inane" work roles to insure "starvation consumer buying" after work, to rescue the decaying human spirit through recreational, creative product, and artistic commodities. This results in equally "crazed" grabbing at "foreign phenomena" (regardless of people who live in different environments and produce alternate products). Voracious hunger expresses itself in aggressive resentment of the uniqueness of others, which imperialists destroy economically, philosophically and militarily at the same time.

Now that conditions of alienational intercultural life have been presented, the reader should ask what she or he can do to alleviate the problem. Peace-making or sanity-preserving suggestions, therefore, will follow, which individually will not revolutionize the world, but *will* contribute to social change.

Individual Peace Initiative #1: Write letters, prepare articles, talk to program and news directors, etc. to encourage media to present an array of documentary, editorial, travel, exposé, historical, economic and political, programming and topical formats (including thought provoking musical selections on radio). These present analyses of international political activities and "relationship problems." This effort includes invitations to local or national experts as presenters or panelists at civic club and organizational functions.

Individual Peace Initiative #2: Organize friends or interested participants (ads in newspapers, church bulletins, community interest T.V. or radio programs, professional journals, etc. can elicit kindred spirits) into small, volunteer, "social action" and learning groups. Then, study the "international peace problem" from a variety of perspectives and initiate action to stimulate broader constituencies. Local and national changes (even if extremely modest) help influence the quality of global life.

Individual Peace Initiative #3: Parents and concerned citizens can communicate in writing, or personally advocate, with boards of education, departments of social and political science at universities, school administrators or individual teachers; for the expansion and improvement of international conflict and peace education. This includes parental "rights" to review contents of textbooks, observe classroom lectures, assist in grant funding for Peace Education initiatives, write or consult regarding the development of Peace Curricula at all grade levels, and encourage teachers to participate in "peace-sensitivity" continuing education.

Individual Peace Initiative #4: A host of "Centers for the Study of Peace" and "Peace Advocacy" organizations throughout the world are desperately seeking volunteers in program operation, financial support and fund-raising, social action, strategic planning, writing, education, etc. This presents an *easy* opportunity to "jump in the mainstream" of peace activities, and also learn from knowledgeable and experienced veterans of this important work: JOIN ONE!!

Individual Peace Initiative #5: For those within bureaucratic or industrial organizations, involvement becomes complicated because of the need to "convert" concepts related to "human essences," "universal compassion," "interpersonal alienation," etc. into pragmatic "conflicts" for organizations, so they are stimulated to change. Individual involvement includes advocacy for "human rights" within organizational policies; suggestions to management of advantages for investing "production monies" in new forms of "human resource development"; or encouragement, of business disengagement from relationships with unethical, alienational, "inhumane" or discriminatory countries or individual companies which exploit humanity.

Individual Peace Initiative #6: Pressure must be placed on congressional leaders through letters, lobbying, voter behavior, media exposure, and political party support, to discourage complacency in overlooking governmental "insanity," insensitivity, and dysfunctional defensiveness/offensiveness—which perpetuates intercultural alienation. Leaders must be stimulated to insist on massive, "rational" and compassionate diplomatic peace initiatives and humanitarian consultation and program development throughout the world. Governments and their business constituencies must precipitate multilateral disarmament, cooperative business ventures, humanitarian aid, expansion of international travel, cessation of weapons manufacture and sales, boycott and ignoring of terrorist acts of revolutionaries (support for global humanitarianism will put these people out of "business"), international resource development and space exploration, and appreciation of human vulnerabilities everywhere. This includes the conversion of military forces and "military manufacturing companies" to "civil service" work forces and "human growth product manufacturers."

Individual Peace Initiative #7: Church and religious/spiritual organizations represent a monumental international "energy" for humanitarian change. The foundation "theories" of love and peace are already in place, and millions of energetic "seekers" and "explorers" currently participate in formal or informal religion throughout the world. They often lack, however, direction for concerted, comprehensive action to put spiritual principles into "practice." Church leaders should be encouraged to combine forces locally and nationally on an interdenominational and intercultural scale, to protest war-inducing governmental and business activities, and supply money, "person-power," and faith/prayer/ inspirational "energy" to global human compassion.

Individual Peace Initiative #8: Talk to everyone you meet, every chance you get, about peace and the insanity of militarism, national defense and war—and *don't shut up* until we fix this "craziness."

Chapter V

MORALITY AND RELIGION

Basic Differentiations

Sensitivity concerning the "truths" of life as expressed, contradicted or ignored by "religion" (scripture, church dogma and *organization,* clergy/ spiritualists, "acts" of nature/humankind, etc.) dictates that this chapter begin with fundamental philosophical, value and definitional premises. In outlining what I do and don't know about "God," religion, and spirituality, "what" I know may be less important to social responsibility and conceptualization of life, than "how" I know, or what I "do not know."

In the first place, humans may be unable to "know that they know" the *pure* nature of "God" or any Supreme Deity or universal ultimate life force. It may be possible, however to actually "know" God, the primordial nature of the universe, the comprehensive essence of "self," etc. In observing the influences of human socialization and personal decision-making: (1) observations *of* the self while it is "knowing," by "the self" or (2) "a" self which must use *socially learned* "concepts" to define what it sees (it sees itself knowing something inside, outside, or the same as its nature); are possibly conditioned by former, present, and future anticipated exigencies of living. We may *never* have a "true" picture of ourselves—even if part of us (mind or body) is perceiving the truth. Although we may "truly" know God, are we "objective" (conflict/fear/anxiety/illusion/ delusion/physiology/status/human need-*free*) enough to *evaluate* the accuracy of this knowledge relative to high probabilities of emotional "indexing" of thoughts? We fall victim to the "illusory" potential of idiosyncratically learned "concepts," which are organizational vehicles with which we conceive other concepts in a chain we cannot observe from outside. We only know what we know by being an integral part of the process, which we may "believe" can remove us from the process (itself), by the formula of its own operation. If anyone *does* directly perceive, intuit, "see" or "know" a God-figure, the knowing could be essentially fulfilling and "complete." Therefore, indulgent descriptions of its occurrence by any part of ourselves which was directly involved, or which differentiated itself secondarily for the "reporting," are impossible or unnecessary. The same principle describes the "truly good" person as unable to discuss their "goodness," which requires the essences of "badness," vanity, pride, etc. which, of course, the "good" person does not possess.

A second "claimer," or disclaimer, is that the unique nature of the human organism exhibits "naturally" superior operational characteristics of neurophysiologic and cognitive-emotional components of being. This includes symbolizing, learning, analyzing and creating/representing/hypothesizing powers. These "processes" provide evidence that, if a "God-figure" *does exist* who/which has *any connection* to initiation, process, or outcome of human life, this "Supreme Entity" intended the quality of life and the interpretive "reality" of universal essence, to be partly a reflection of the complex computer system known as "homo sapiens." Although the nature of a potential Supreme Being has its own entity, the "specialness of personhood" tells us that "God" can and must be "known" as part of humans "knowing themselves." In this regard, human history exemplifies a progressive and multidimensional "pyramidal energy movement" of exploratory, stimulus-seeking, reconciliational, hierarchical and "architectural" style; which seeks integration and acquisition of "holistic reality" (inner plus outer). In the context of this search, we seem instinctually programmed to "appreciate" our own essence within every problem-solving task pursued. Therefore, "what" God "is" should be, by design, what man and woman also "is." "Truth" subsumes "validity attributes" which the truth-knower maintains as internally consistent, honest, current, sensitive, comprehensive, intensified, etc., processes of engaging the truth—whatever its "true" nature. In this regard, any God "is" partly what the perceivers "are." Society has no "authorization" to differentiate quality of any *behavioral* self, or the *God-perceiving* self, relative to overarching dogmas concerning the true nature and will of God. This God, furthermore, "seems" to have "created" an extraordinary "apparatus" which is intended for use, in its apparently "imperfect" or fully human form. We are at least one vehicle which cannot be used to know its originator by not "knowing" itself, which we apparently also cannot "not know," to some extent.

Thirdly, spiritual or religious canons insist on the "superiority" of the empyrean or "quinte-centric creator." The logical assumption, therefore, to contradict arrogant proclivities of "humanoidism," is that there is no reason to assume that human cognition can rationalize, deduce, or comprehend the dynamic nature or comprehensive functioning of any God-figure. The ability of "the created" to use inferior characteristics to "understand" the creator, suggests a "transcendence in knowing" even beyond the capacities of the God. This process of objectifying "Her, His, or Its" attributes and systemic relationships with other preeminent beings or collateral energies/substances, leads to the following possibilities:

1. The "created" are actually superior to the "creator" but do not know it. This negates concepts of original creation and superiority because a God would assumedly know itself.

2. The Creator "needs" appreciative understanding from its "subjects," which negates, again, the power of a "superior essence." If truly superior, God would not program "needs" into its essence and would find limited human awareness extremely deficient, which could have been "adjusted upward" with original "blueprints" of life.

3. The creator and created are equal. This suggests no need for "horizontal differentiation" of the Supreme-Self except to compensate for some deficiency, which "should" not exist within the essence of the Master-Architect.

4. God is developmentally "above" human nature with hierarchical creative abilities. God also occupies an inferior sequential position relative to an even higher power, which is beyond observational or conceptual ranges of linear subunits of an ultimate but "discriminable" supreme power.

5. The creator can "achieve" increasing levels of awareness and understanding through cognitive and emotional skills, and diminution of human forms of ineptness (fear, delusion, selfishness, etc.). There are serious questions of the value of this "game" to the "manufacturer," who knows the outcome and would not, ostensibly, need humble *gains* of the human race to compensate celestial deficiency. This justifies inability, using human logic, to *ever* understand "divine logic," which seems not to need "benefits" of human logic to fulfill its destiny.

In considering the absence of a "Supreme Force" altogether, reconstructed anthropologic and archaeologic histories of evolution have meticulously traced primate development as a separate category of linear progression (it doesn't look like we came *directly* or *most immediately* from fish, rocks, plants, etc.). Also, qualitative and experimental research supports a substantive "gap" in evolutionary progression. This separates homo sapiens as having "leaped ahead" through catastrophic crisis or stimulant force of mega-proportions, or suggests a separate origin of humans as distinct from antecedent and parallel "brothers and sisters" in the ape family. Primary differentiation of humans is "extrinsic symbolization" (conceptual, abstract, self-observational, analytic thinking) and development of "culture" (collective norms, negotiated interactive systems, cooperative emotional reciprocity, "collective consciousness," etc.). These suggest (1) an eco-cosmically unique heritage and destiny, with decidedly superior powers relative to coexistent "life forms," that (2) did not "emerge" from common genetic survival formulas. Also, (3) this cannot be explained relative to intricacy of bio-psycho integration (mind and body interaction) and autonomous motivational capacities (the ability of men and women to "decide") by theories of physics, cosmic energy, solar perturbation, nuclear production, etc. We have a unique and separate "cause" which presently, and possibly perpetually, we are unable to explain. In this vein, we are unable to *definitively* connect principles of "morality" to those of "causal destiny," which I will discuss more fully as this chapter unfolds.

My fifth point, is that religion or spirituality, and organized social institutions of either one, are not necessarily synonymous. Churches appear *not* to represent direct truths of morality, nor the "precise" nature of God's plan under the following conditions:

1. Churches are "ordained" by a Supreme Deity, wherein "qualitative requisites" of human life are presented at *different* times and locations throughout history.

2. Communicational channels include "human conductors" who, though potentially "inspired," maintain latitude in interpretive revelation of central ideas.

3. Codes of "Holy" teaching are maintained and disseminated through a myriad of cultural "processes" that have influenced church as well as secular organizations throughout history.

4. The constituents and leaders of religious institutions are, in fact, *inferior* to the sovereignty of a real or symbolized deity. Competent practice of religion requires "developmental" advancement through stages of hierarchical status where "deficiencies" are recognized within the human "transcending status."

Principles of moral or religious life, of course, may be delivered outside, or "in spite of," functional dynamics and "consciousness-shaping" characteristics of social systems. Also, there are violations and deviancies of representatives, members, and operational activities of religious institutions, in affirmed contradictions to their own avowed normative standards. Although many dimensions of "church life" may, indeed, express linear and unmitigated articulations of "God's intents," diviations suggest they categorically cannot be construed as unequivocal parallels in every principle of faith. In differentiating religion from spirituality, "canonized" practices of worship, faith and evangelistic action may be genuine examples of psycho-emotional "connective linkages" between creator and created. These practices may be specified by Supreme Authority, in whatever form, or may only be "legitimately" authorized by person-kind. Procedural compliance with thought "presentation," emotional intensification or demeanor, or behavioral repertoire, may represent spirituality in its traditional and "thoroughbred" form. This may or may not require specific motivational, attitudinal, or conceptual "nuances of cognition." However, idiosyncratic expressions of the self-in-relationship-to-God, or self-in-alienation-to-God, or self-neutral-to-God, may ramify as "non-spiritual" expressions of socio-religious protocol. Some form of ultra-spirituality, may surpass lesser degrees of "fervor-of-the-soul." "Ultraness" may "elevate" any particular personality into a richer spiritual domain. This "place" may reflect individual existence or a "contextual partnership" with the essence of the "universal energy," defined as the prime cause and/or focus of the "centrality" of life. Also, numerous psychologic, sociologic, historical and anthropologic writings discuss (1) "culture-coded" forms of gender/family/tribe or subgroup/personality spiritual "awareness," (2) psychophysiologic configuration of the "self," which seem spiritual, (3) altered states of consciousness, and (4) ritualized ceremonial "status," etc. The aforementioned have been *correlated* statistically and conceptually to numerous *non-spiritual demographics* (e.g., gender, parenting, ecology, perceptual orientation, personality style, etc.). There is, also, evidence to link "journeys of the spiritual self" to forms of *social conditioning* or even pathogenic *emotional trauma*, although some states of psychic expression have not, as yet, been secularized relative to cause-effect etiology. Expressions of cultural spiritual practices may, conversely, represent "hallowed" and theocratically inspired states of spiritualism whose manifestation can only be expressed/accented via interpersonal "convections" of collective energy.

The last point (#6, for those counting) concerns not the nature of God, person, spiritualism, or religion, but the human *process* we undertake to reach conclusions about the "correct" natures of the above phenomena. Through typologies of rhetoric, persuasive argument, authoritative mandate, emotional dramatization, collective group action, rationalistic deduction, impassioned plea, analytic observation, or manipulative contrivance; people will possibly *never* achieve irrefutable "proof" of the existence or nonexistence of a "Supreme Being or Phenomenon." If proof does emerge, this essence may not (1) meet all our needs and expectations, (2) provide infinite justification for the trials and tribulations of life, (3) signify a specialized "relationship" with any one of us, (4) validate cultural "decisions" about the best ways to conduct the "business" of life, or (5) guarantee retribution/remuneration for negatives or positives we encounter relative to goodness/badness or other qualitative aspects of "being." Where "proof" emerges as a result of human *interaction,* there are reasonable grounds to doubt the "independence" of any manifestation of human dialectic and judgment. Autonomy in this case concerns the questionable ability of the mind to extract its "vulnerable nature" from the confinements of its own history, development, cultural training, psycho-defensive posturing—to arrive at unencumbered visions of the "ultimate truth" (or lack thereof). As we explore superordinate "essences," most of us, unfortunately, will have (1) preeminated facts or operating principles we will accept, to justify paths we have already chosen or been "assigned" (in our minds), or we will (2) ratify principles which "fit" the skills and motivational paradigms we feel we can implement to get on board the "Last Train For Clarksville." Most discussions of "truth" eliminate opportunities to learn or experience the phenomenon in question, because the mind, once engaged in productive activity, offers little opportunity for conflicting reality. Its natural movement occurs between concepts it already knows, and as long as it "demonstrates" its knowing, probably cannot "know" anything new. Since most of us don't really listen much, or precipitate crises in concretized belief systems, the *irrelevancy* of *ways* we "engage" each other to learn about God or anything else, may mean that truth truly learned, will be destroyed the moment humans talk about it.

Goodness vs. Badness

Distinctions between bipolarizations of a continual range of human, and presumably divine, characteristics, are difficult to discuss. This is true if we focus on innate natures of "valuated behavior," rather than conjecturing about "causes" or degrees of "potency" within categories. The simplest approach is to pass judgment on various holders of these titles as "different" from ourselves. Discussions of goodness and badness are usually subsumed "naturally" within the right-wrong, conforming-deviant rubric of "morality," which is furthermore subsumed as an important principle of "Divine Dominion." Assuming that God or any Divine Power is also a "moral" authority, however, can be questioned from numerous contradictory standpoints. The "interpretational" and "cultural" influences on Holy scripture, and the symbolic and seemingly intermittent nature of Divine intervention, make God's morality hard to pin down. With this "conditional" assumption about the true authorship and destiny of moral functions and precepts, we can "break down" the discussion into several sub-points which clarify the debate.

Phenomenal Essence

The condition of either "good" or "bad" humanhood, is supposedly identified through empirical "behavioral" observation. Definitions, however describe a set of *cognitively derived conclusions* about *interpersonal* reality, which relates to "hurtful" outcomes for "victims." The "formula" in the good or bad "perpetrator's" mind usually relates to "material" giving or receiving actions. But, it presupposes a concept of "self" which does or does not recognize a universal "truth" of the basic values of dignity, self-determination, or need-fulfillment. The concept of "other" seems differentiated from "self," although may be only a symbolized "reflection" of varying fulfilled or deprived conditions of self-adequacy. A good or bad "person," therefore, sees the "self" as excessively needy or fulfilled, where interactions with others become direct reflections of need-satisfaction in terms of economic notions of *gains* or *losses*. The "bad" person who takes from others (property, self-respect, life, etc.) is fulfilling a need in self; just as the "giving" person satisfies internal demands for dispersion of excess baggage (extra love to give) or corrects deficits in desired feelings ("I give and feel better about myself when I do so"). In terms of "adding" to or "subtracting" from the self, in cases of verbal or attitudinal interchanges with others, the recipient of the moral or immoral intention must "receive" the input relative to their perceptions of themselves ("My feelings were *not* hurt because I chose not to feel deprived relative to comments from others"). This "validates" the nature of the act, although morality of intentions can also be judged without an actual, corporeal recipient—the principles are the same. In cases of physical giving or taking, "outcomes" steal center stage focus, when causal concepts prior to results are ignored, or categorically judged as negative or positive, relative to gains/losses of the victim/beneficiary.

The essence of "morality" relates directly to "mathematically quantified" *amounts* or *substances* of valued commodities (property, attention, respect, love) which we believe "actually" are "exchanged" between people. Basic motivations, however, for outward signs come from neuro-electrical impulses that produce chemically bioenergized cellular configurations of matter in the brain. Outcomes at the atomic level, do not appear to exist as either right or wrong "units of electricity." They are labeled as identity attributes relative to the juxtaposition and need-hierarchy nature of the symbolic concepts—particularly when expressed interpersonally. With no "moral" or "immoral" forms of brain electricity per se, differentiated perceptions of need-deprivation/fulfillment, are what remains. Scientists still cannot locate these "things" we lose or gain, although our communicational symbol systems have been constructed to make us believe we "have" or "have not," which predisposes decisions to interact according to this acquisitional frame of reference.

In cases of immoral or moral behavior which represent social or religious rule violation (adultery, profanity, vanity, etc.) or compliance (heroism, fidelity, humility), the basic nature of "morality-indexed relevancy" derives its rationale from the category of *behavior itself*. We exclude the implicit *motivations* behind anyone's performance of acts. Where particular behaviors maintain continuity throughout history, we assume that their "staying power" necessarily validates their truth, as mandatory prescriptions for life. This "sustenance" depends on degree of conformity or deviance, and places the behaver in "conditions of being" at some future time ("Heaven" and "Hell" usually). In the "hereafter," attributes of this state of the self are depicted relative to feelings or emotions (or exaggerations thereof) which can *only* correspond to experiences we have encountered in past or present emotional life. These are identical types of feelings experienced by those conforming, or violating norms. Humans can only "be human" until they "rise above" or "transcend" humanity. Good or bad behavior is performed because humans seek present or future emotional experiences they "know about," which can only be "known" presently, relative to what is "already known." This "justification" process raises serious questions of whether people can "perceive" the Divine, on issues of morality or anything else. Also, can *any* self be "extracted" from emotion-stimulating existence, to logically view "implications" of actions whose outcomes are still defined in terms of human emotion? Can categorical definition of behavior, which must be caused by emotional need, "intersect" this human process of emotional need-satisfaction? Also, can we subdefine any *part* of this feeling continuum as either "good or bad," when humanly perceived emotion is the alpha and omega of the pattern?

In cases where a God-figure has "truly" ordained "good" or "bad" behavior manifestations, several issues remain unclear:

1. Why has the repertoire of human emotions not been differentiated to correspond to "morality relevancies," so we are not trapped in doing bad "things" for good reasons (satisfaction of "normal" emotion) or good things for bad reasons (which are "good" reasons if the perpetrator is filling the self with positive emotions)?

2. Why are emotion and cognition not more fully "integrated" so that cognitive understanding can override feeling? This delimma paradoxically contradicts conceptualizations of the "spiritual soul."

3. Why must emotion be such a predominant "natural" ingredient of human dependency (from birth onward) that to ignore or transcend emotion, becomes anti-human?

Concerning moral contingencies and social pragmatism, the capability of human ingenuity to change social life, given declinations of ecological resources, suggests that "adaptation" must necessarily *change* if survival is to be insured. Adaptive capability is necessary if reproductive genetic attributes *are* to be rational "standard equipment." This is true even from a Divine creator who "appears" to have little reason for constituting a phenomena that would negate itself rather than change ("regressive creationism" seems incongruent). Also, if human modification of subsistence patterns and corresponding lifestyles was not "intended," the environment (1) would remain constant (which it does not), (2) would provide inexhaustible resource energies (which it also does not), or (3) humans would be more controlled by equally powerful predators. Reproduction would not represent (1) significant levels of instinctual drive, or (2) personal choice with the "choosing minds" we have inherited—if "change" is a mandated "blueprint" of human existence. Alteration of all forms of behaving, thinking and feeling seems unavoidable at worst, absolutely necessary at best, and suggests that "laws" about the "good of society" must innately possess flexibility. Such capacity is also mandated by technology, economics, aesthetics, medicine, nutrition, transportation, and communication, as they force culture to undergo modification and reconstruction to insure survival and "progress" of a species. This is particularly true with species that reproduce in massive proportions, use up resources, symbolize spiritual and social relevancy, and increase in capacity for independent decision-making prior to senescence. "Moral" evaluations of lifestyle, therefore, appear to be conservative and counterproductive resistances to normal patterns of "forward" movement, or at least non-static movement. While intended to accent the highest virtues of life itself, morality may necessarily negate a large portion of this life by superimposing a "still life picture of one essence" on top of a moving panorama which is an integral part of that essence.

Lastly, if morality is a condition of "somethingness" existent in the "mind" of God, it is uncertain how human interpretation of its nature or consequences can have assurance of accuracy, unless the mind of God is like the mind of humankind. "We" may be all that "is," or God may be much less capable than most of us want to assume. This also questions the metaphorical nature of historical theological communications from "on High." Hereby, a superior "being" manifests "sub-trospecting" conceptions of "qualitative being-ness" to fit within inferior realms of human cognition. It implies an overarching benefit to the moral discovery "process." The implication also follows that God intends, therefore, distortions of interpretation as we learn what is "right" and "wrong." This negates the need for any of us to tell any of us what "is" moral, because God intended for us not to know now/fully/altogether/yet. Another option is to have been told the "truth" directly (or known it all along), which raises the question of benefit for the creator to "plant seeds" of wisdom, rather than simply produce the "whole enchilada." In sum, (1) the interpretation of superordinate phenomena, (2) by subordinate interpreters whose experience is a (3) progressive exposure to hierarchical levels of that phenomenon, (4) when they have inferior "cognating" and "emoting" equipment with which to (5) not-know ultimate truth unless they are equal to the creator, who would (6) not be the creator of *equal* creatures—suggests we all be very careful in deciding, beyond a shadow of a doubt, what is *right* or *wrong*, or *how to live life qualitatively!*

Pleasure

Morality publicly centers itself on social, psychological and spiritual "consequences" of deviant behavior:

1. Consequences represent "presumed or experienced" negative social *impacts* ("forecast" in the future, based on previous observations of people, rather than the "immorals" in question), or *projections* taken from religious dogma in the form of literary or ritualized tradition. The underlying values are assumed to be humanly objective, divinely inspired, or verbatim from God. We simultaneously affirm our inevitable subjective natures, and "believe" in Divine Inspiration because others have advised us about the truth.

2. Consequences represent psychological "losses," which are adjudged by someone other than the actual "loser."

3. Consequences represent "psychic affronts" to those who believe differently, and decide that the quality of *our* "intent" is tarnished by dissonant actions of someone else. This occurs despite the fact that many believe God "relates directly" to every person, and establishes a communal connection with humanity at large.

4. Consequences represent degradation to a Supreme Power, who "needs" the "support" of inferior mortals. This "projection" to God of our vulnerabilities, lessens fear of control or retribution, boosts our needs for "equivalency," and "familiarizes" us with a phenomenon we feel very inept at understanding. We furthermore believe this Supreme Power possesses a "mechanism" to receive "emotional" stimuli from subordinates. God contains decision-making formulas which actually "register" notations of status, relative to Divine "standards" of normative "dimensions" of sensation or essence.

Negative consequences *promised* to "errant" human-kind, or *earned,* are very interesting. As a matter of fact, the notion of achieving "just deserts" is a concept itself, that relates to *human* systems of bartering, monetary exchange, parent-child power debates, and behavior reinforcement theory. Achievement does not necessarily translate directly, or at all, into operational frameworks of divine matrices of spiritual cause and effect. Consequences, symbolically, are conceptualized relative to existing perceptions of pain, fear, loss, emptiness, or confusion, to which humans (but not Gods, necessarily) assign negative and avoidant labels. However, smaller degrees of worldly pain, per se, are not "bad." This pain is associated with grammatical "bad" adjectives when perceived in the "beyond world." That which is "unpleasant but not bad" when it is experienced but not understood, becomes an outcome of "bad" when anticipated for a future no one can "know" now. Yet, the smaller doses presently experienced are not considered consequences of previous "bads" which we also cannot "know," because the past is equally nonexistent, with the future. Badness, then, is associated with a "pleasure-pain" continuum which contains some universal "registry" or accounting framework. In this case, any particular behavior "becomes" a symbolic or "actual" recorded tabulation, with a "being status" defined as "displeasing" to a Supreme Entity. There is an assumption, also, that "pleasure" can be understood as awareness, intent, perception, position, movement, etc. on the part of the Creator. However, we *cannot know* God in "true form," but *must know* this being to associate our behavioral consequences to "their" (its, Her, His) identity dimensions. We think recorded accounts can actually *be* recorded accounts. With this complexity, of course, one would question why "God" would (1) create an unknowing constituency, then (2) go to the trouble of simplifying and translating everything into insufficient mental frameworks, which means that (3) our "outcomes" must be transposed again into the Divine framework. The aforementioned are a lot of steps to "improve the inadequate" to a status they could have *begun* with. "Perfection," also, should not need reward or punishment of "soulful essences" which reflect the "goodness" or natural essence of the creator. In this context, the Creator would possess differential hierarchies of quality in order to produce regressively (make an inferior product). What is the *advantage* of a "Perfect Being's" perception of imperfection?

Back to the human realm, immorality, is signatured with an assumption of "pleasure" with the "forbidden," which is an extremely indeterminate concept in and of itself. Pleasure, as an emotion, cannot be empirically verified except through referential behavior indicators which are culturally, but not phenomenally "validated" (what is a smile, really?). Certainly pleasure has not been definitively "separated out" from various aspects of chemo-physiology, nor has emotion been understood as a nonphysical or spiritual entity by psychologic or parapsychologic scientists. Pleasure may represent (1) reduction of pain or anxiety, (2) return of the "excited" organism to a baseline resting condition, or (3) intensification of psychophysiology. In many instances, immoral labels suggest "exaggerations" of excitations or relaxations, which means that everyone is immoral, but to differing degrees. Also, applications of normal "degrees of pleasure" to situations which are "nontraditional," confuse the basic perspective on moral or immoral. In this sense, *inherent* human characteristics (e.g., tension reduction, body contact, emotional intensification, etc.) represent a continuum which, at one geometric point in time, converts one essential characteristic (good) to its opposite:

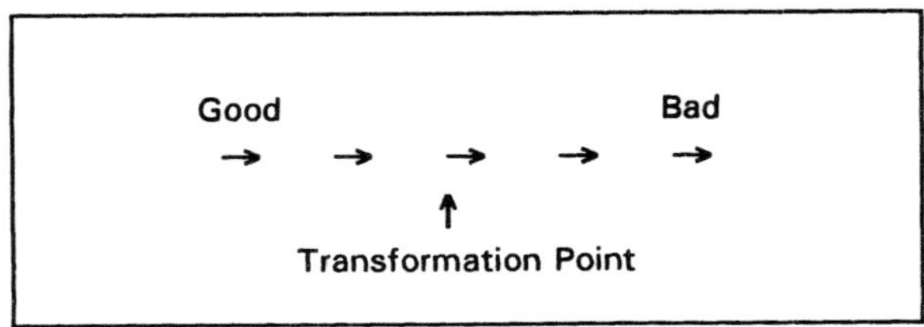

When electrical activity or molecular body movement is considered in its nuclear atomic structure, it would appear impossible to differentiate one diametric position from another, or to even *view* the linear chain of benchmarks in psychology, spirituality or physiology. Consider inputs from any of us into the intersecting phenomenal realms of moral and immoral:

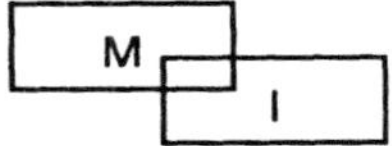

How do we decide at which existential point we traversed the critical boundary? On the other hand, if overarching concrete outcomes rather than gradations of perception and motivation are considered, several questions emerge: (1) Is there immoral behavior without immoral intent (e.g., mentally retarded person's "sin")? (2) How do positive intents (love) intersect with "negative" outcomes (love someone of the same gender sexually)? (3) How does "pure" physiology (two sets of skin molecules touching) *actually* (microscopic or macroscopic levels) formulate bioenergetic essence into abstract categories of "rightness" or "wrongness"? From a mezzo level, obviously, behaviors can be differentiated, but at which level of specificity or comprehensiveness does God view life?

Another perspective about "pleasure," of course, is need-satisfaction discussed earlier. All acts may simply represent the illusion of "filling" an empty psycho-emotional space. If any "self" perceives itself to be partly or largely "empty," it probably cannot also perceive itself as capable of non-deprivational decision-making. This is true because (1) the choice of an alternate moral option (from an immoral one) (2) necessarily forces the "chooser" into a position of threatened power and vulnerability (A is not a free choice if consequences are attached, but is a "mandated non-choice"), so that (3) the very act of "choosing" means one is deprived and needy. This suggests (1) reduced power to choose, (2) minimal credibility for the actual positive selection, and (3) reduced ability to "search" the environment for a more adequate choice. It also places the person in a deprivation-resolved status after the choice, where they cannot even perceive the same "self" before or after the choice.

Righteousness

"Morality" (moral, immoral, anti-moral or non-moral) is "focused" in one of the following ways:

1. Morality is a category of behaviors precipitated by pleasure/pain.

2. Morality has social/religious consequences of "targeted" behaviors or represents an inherent God-alien/antithetic nature.

3. Morality is positive or negative as a "spiritual" consequence, for the perpetrators of variously labeled acts.

Those who occupy formal or informal "moral authority" roles, appear to also assign human/worldly statuses of righteousness, holiness, etc. to various acts. These assignments categorize qualities of "intent of motivation" which functions to transform or "pro-evolve" some dimensions of human nature into anticipated realms of Divine nature/essence. They simultaneously pinpoint portions of the Divine, which already exist in "secular" personas of worldly life. As "righteousness" is further examined, there are several aspects which "apparently" contradict some ostensible precepts of collectively "known" cultural interpretations of morality and qualitative life:

1. Righteousness suggests conformity to "Divinely mandated" or authorized principles of living, which (a) restrict definitions of "pure love," (b) contain "situational" contingencies which reverse the categorical nature of specific behaviors (killing for right and wrong reasons), (c) do not specifically index many physical behaviors, themselves, as isolated reflections of righteous essence (touching per se, as opposed to who is touched, when, and under what social circumstances), (d) have a "cultural" interpretation.

2. Righteousness suggests absolute compliance with pre-existing rules, and extreme "dependency" on authoritative control from a "Supreme Leadership

Function." These "teachers" contradict capabilities, motivations and values of autonomy and independent decision-making (righteousness does not allow opportunity or capability to "choose" non-righteousness).

3. Common definitions of righteousness exclude rationales for individual good ideations as an "integrated function" with other emotions. Self-perceived need-deprivation, as a motivation for selecting a "good deed" to fulfill one's emptiness, psychologically, does not transfer "human deficit conditions" into "divine asset conditions" with any formula for evaluation.

4. Despite omniscient, omnipresent, and omnipotent characteristics of "God-heads," culture insists on gross indices of evaluative outcomes, and makes decisions about the "-eousness" of "right." Conversely, idiosyncratic cognitive manifestations of intensity, direction, symbolic representation, genre, unification, etc. are virtually ignored despite their role as prime energy sources to "acquire" states of being.

5. The issue of the "self's" "knowing" that it is righteous is rarely discussed, relative to the following:

    a. the potentially "negating nature" of directly observing the self performing externally direct acts (they are "not what they are" if we are watching ourselves simultaneously);

    b. the possibility of self-indulgent "knowing" of self-righteousness as an example of human need to *artificially* validate, which, of course, invalidates righteousness the moment we "name" righteousness to fill unrighteous voids in selfhood; or

    c. the "conscious selection" of goal-directed righteous behavior which presupposes an "ulterior" motive (or else why choose in the first place) that:

        (1) removes the "essence of the righteousness" to a symbolic set of interactions *elsewhere* outside the self,

        (2) mitigates the "purity" of the righteous act,

        (3) reinforces cognitive consonance of supporting the "choice" of the choosing process, which removes alternate choices from "possibility" and, diminishes the quality of that which, by familiarity and conditioning, is not fully or even really "chosen,"

(4) reduces universal focus from being-with-God/Self/Ultimacy, etc., to environmentally distracting conditions that control the physical self at the expense of the psychic or spiritual self,

d. the destruction of "perfect righteousness" with "conception" which (1) necessarily reduces "holistic reality" into discriminative subdimensions which, to apply human decision-making, must necessarily (2) alter the original essence of any natural or supernatural entity, which (3) moves the perceiver to a status of prejudicial and circumscriptive conduct to the extent that (4) thinking ultimately prevents knowing, and knowing ultimately prevents "perfect being."

Ideology and Defense

"Beliefs" about morality, God, religion or spirituality serve a variety of human "needs," irrespective of the actual natures of supernatural phenomena. This does not, necessarily, suggest personal pathology or abnormal tendency to "construct" particular dimensions of reality, or ultra-reality (although exaggerated inclinations may represent deviance, illness, maladjustment, etc.). The vulnerable and dependent human condition, serves as a "natural" foundation for the evolution of thought patterns and associated behaviors which function in the following ways:

1. Thoughts and behaviors recapitulate childhood experiences which were comfortable, or they resolve conflicts which created fear and anxiety then, and manifest symbolic "compensations" now. The conscious mind struggles to wrestle control of identity from the unguarded, honest, selfish, fearful selves. These perpetually dwell in the unconscious, where their seeds were planted as a result of uncontrollable childhood experiences.

2. Thoughts and behaviors respond to inherent or learned "energies" of the bio-sensory system which seeks stimulation. These alternate with regressive processes to return to homeostatic "resting" conditions, plus provide enticements to learn concepts, master the environment, explain phenomena, and "feel emotion."

3. Thoughts and behaviors negotiate functional relationships with other people, which provide data about the "relevance" of the self. They establish networks of "reciprocity" of obligation, cooperation, evaluation, problem-solving and self-explanation (all the world's a stage), or aggrandizement (a disguised form of aggrandizement is victimization).

4. Thoughts and behaviors conform (excessive deviation is another form of dependency and disguised conformity) to social standards of public accomplishment, self-improvement, behavioral predictability, controlled or sublimated violence, loyalty and optimism.

The problem with the central, natural or appropriate roles of religion, spirituality, morality, etc., is that the human "developmental" pattern is characterized by anomalies and itinerant contradictions. External standards of evaluative feedback about any "condition of the self" are subjectively perceived by the "selves" that are being evaluated. Also, models of comprehensive criterial validation are constituted by personalities that maintain vested interests in the constitutional "truth" of logical templates of reality so developed. Some anomalies are as follows:

1. The ultimate conclusion of human life on earth is "loss," yet life is characterized relative to a variety of "gains"—which suggests illogic in human decision-making (or the overriding design of life).

2. "Qualitative" life is constituted by development and utilization of mental symbolic concepts. They are "invisible" to common observation. Yet they are strangely utilized as "validating precepts" for a multitude of qualitative states of society or self, especially concerning "moral and ethical" concerns.

3. Humans exist in a physiologic state of extreme vulnerability, always a "breath" or "heartbeat" away from death, yet survive by developing creative ways to personally and publicly deny this "reality."

4. Humans have extraordinary capacity for memory and learning, yet demonstrate conservative, redundant, and counterproductive compulsively rigid behaviors and "thought clusters."

5. The value of life is described by earthly humanity, and "communicated" by God (directly or through interpretation) as positive, good, "humane," etc. This happens despite "apparently" horrible presence of human suffering, destruction, and "senseless" tragedy.

6. Life is characterized by necessary "dependencies," yet the struggle most articulated by experts on growth and development, is the quest for personal independence, or healthy reciprocal dependence.

7. The mind seems naturally divided into conscious and unconscious components, plus various functional ego processes. However, venerated ancient and modern spiritualists, *diligently avow* the need for personality

unification, integration, centeredness, oneness, peace, holism, etc. This contradicts the natural or "unnaturally learned" patterns of "normal" development.

With these aspects of "life" and "self" in mind, it is time to consider various roles "assumed" or "assigned" relative to *moral ideology*, which, play significant parts in the confusing patterns just described.

Moral Ideology Role #1: Self-Enhancement: Moral principles are "subsumed" within the umbrella "jurisdiction" of some "heavenly Kingdom" or "God-Realm." The corresponding inclination of men and women who occupy roles of sycophantic ministration, is to authoritatively *judge* the attitudes and behaviors of others. These evaluations concern "ethereal norms" within "abstract domains" of "trans-existent" (being human and responsible for divine accountability simultaneously) "multiple realities." This suggests a benefit to be gained by the "judger," who otherwise should have little capability to assess anyone else. Their "mission" of ecumenism should, most logically, entail assistance to others to "unify" with a deity, to enhance ability for effective self-evaluation. In this scenario, God knows that self-evaluation will not be improved in the human mental configuration by processes of blame or negative judgment. The judgment of others, by using "elevated" standards that are not empirically verifiable allows all of us to assume superiority. We enhance the "necessarily inferior" self, by attacking qualitative characteristics of lesser magnitude in others. More directly, we use abstract concepts of "ultimate hierarchies" of status (honor, dignity, holiness, purity) to escalate perceptions of the "ordinary" nature of humanity, into conditions of greater importance. This is particularly true when society defines specific dimensions of worldly importance which, at various or recurrent times, any one of us may *not* achieve. Concepts from "other realities" can be moved, expanded, contracted, energized, brightened, etc. more easily than visible, behaviorally-anchored "testimonial" symbols. These ultimately decline anyway, as death approaches.

Moral Ideology Role #2: Personal Differentiation: In a parallel process to "aggrandizement of vulnerable identity," (1) similarities we share as "natural animals," (2) common "needs" which comfort us, but raise questions of "why me?" when the person next door "seems relatively equivalent," and (3) pressures everyone experiences to expand mental capacities; all propel a search for "uniqueness" and "unit-indexing" of each self. Children "force" themselves away from controlling parents by proving they (the child-self) are *not* mom or dad. Adolescents and young adults, too, "separate" as they learn complex patterns of interpersonal reciprocity, to share common goals and characteristics. They interweave differences so that dyadic couplings become "stronger" through accumulated diversities which fill voids in the partner, and accent need-meeting intentions of each "giving self." There is expansion of personality attributes, feelings, perceptions, "senses," values, and "presences" into an expansive world of universal animation, vivication, signification, etc. This extrapolation allows any self to (1) believe its mind has an enormous inner dimension of variable function and operation, but also (2) validate this "differentiation" as representing actually different "selves" within the same "self" that exists in a vast "cafeteria" of "selectable options." Multiplicity of choice lets us believe (3) there is progressive "purpose" and continuing value to a comprehensive existence.

Moral Ideology Role #3: Comprehensive "Undoing": We all carry a burden of powerless and anxiety-ridden childhood *inadequacy*. This burden is transported unconsciously and consciously into adulthood as an *integral belief* that the self has basic "flaws," which must be "reversed" or at least redirected. There is debate, of course, about whether the self is strong, weak, progressive, regressive, or cannot be qualitatively assessed by any criteria. Typical developmental attitudes, however, ignore this existential question, and characteristically define the self as (1) "deficient" in attributes, (2) having a fundamentally "good or bad" nature, (3) able to be manipulated in categories of thought/emotion, and (4) behaviorally conforming to rules which extend from natural life into the celestial beyond. The "self" fails to achieve different types or degrees of predetermined or situational goals, depending on amount of pressure any of us experiences, and the relevance of goal attainment to aspects of "quality self." We may perceive "failure" or "inadequacy" of the personality, which represents, socially, the inability to attain symbolized artifacts of "success" through conformity to cultural prerequisite behaviors. Psychologically, this translates into the recollected and unconsciously reactivated "sensation of loss" of parental love and associated protection/nurturance. It also translates into concomitant inability to control parents, which the child's mind connects with a status of undesirability of the self/being. The child in us fears (and remembers) retaliative losses of nurturance, physical comfort, or even identity itself.

Because of social and physical barriers in all phases of life, the easiest and most reliable methods of "correcting human deficit" are as follows:

1. Espouse beliefs which exist *independent* of the controls of humanity, and are accessed privately without cooperative effort or "local authorization" from competitors.

2. Develop hierarchies of belief that contain differential quality dimensions to offset cultural negative judgement, and various depths of human despair or depression.

3. Reiterate unconscious needs for parental affirmation of relevance per se, through global and esoteric beliefs about the world. Ideology allows a "start fresh" because of a "higher principle" that overrides a subsidiary norm. It constitutes an "ultimate perspective" with a wider vision of the "total self" than do authority figures of "earthly circumscription." Ideology is also authorized by a Supreme Power that provides a "stamp of assurance" on whatever we believe, and removes the "game of life" from a high loss-probability domain. We can (1) be "forgiven," (2) "start over again" without a weighted history or negative "legacy," (3) believe we are given strength or assistance beyond the normal supply with which we have "failed," (4) fantasize an inter-"personal" alliance to combat loneliness and provide connection, and (5) conceptualize a new horizon where past negative events are no longer "accumulated."

Moral Ideology Role #4: Displacement of Anger: There is a frustrating problem of growth and development, which accompanies the self's struggle for independence from parental (later excessive personal) controls. It is related to resentment for our vulnerable "need" for dependent nurturance and protection from others. This problem is *anger* in the psychodynamic system. As part of frustrated need-deprivation (anger) we experience toward authority and resource-controlling figures, we are "cornered" with reluctance to express anger, and alienate future suppliers of gratifications we desire. In this entrapment, substitutes must be found who are "inferior" to us, which is actually *our* fear of *their* superiority, autonomy, or pleasure. We need an "explanatory framework" to justify the self-perceived (unconscious) irrationality and destructiveness of anger, which threatens to confirm our learned identities as "bad" selves. Negative identities hidden by anger also contradict the values of personal worth, unification, and positiveness which we desire in idealized, conflict-free lives. The use of moral "domains" as battlefields and idealized "ratifiers" (in the "persona" of God as Divine "Parental" figurehead) of our "justified wrath," allows symbolic functions related to "just" anger:

1. We symbolize anger at the "parent-child dilemma" by categorizing others as deviant within a world (the celestial firmament) where they (a) may not even identify themselves as "actors," yet (b) cannot defend their identities because we, the "plaintiffs," are "tuned-in" to a spiritual "program" which only we and God truly understand.

2. We freely judge and attack "sinners" as a way of ridding our "teapots" of excessive steam.

3. We symbolize our "dependent natures" through adherence to commands from "On High."

4. We deal with anger at our own perceived weaknesses by identifying this aspect of "vulnerable humanity" in others. We attack them rather than ourselves, for which we believe we will receive parental approval from various regions of Divine Hierarchy.

Moral Ideology Role #5: Rationalization: To survive and confirm beliefs (illusions, delusions, fantasies or truths) of our "relevance," we experience life as a multi-ingredient "stew." This stew contains events, ideas, actions, etc. that impact each other as a result of continuous "boiling" sensory, physical, emotional and spiritual "energies." We "stir in" mental and emotional processes of planning, decision-making, reasoning, explaining, etc. to arrange inner concepts in a balanced and functionally organized system of need-satisfactions. In the "ferment" of this lifelong task of orienting the "self" to itself and others, unexplainable, disruptive, and confusing, "happenings" fill our lives, which create conflict and anxiety to the psychic system. We develop beliefs (supported by culture) in logical, inductive-deductive linear reasoning, which have no "concept content" to integrate explanations of many of our own "failures," poor decisions, misunderstandings, rejections, etc. Rather than accepting responsibility for these "dissonant" events, which we can neither analyze "correctly" nor reverse completely, we reach for the heavens as the undeniable realm of holistic, comprehensive, and more broadly rational conceptualization of the world. At this ulterior level, *all* events have a "higher," more "complex" or more "pure" meaning. This meaning is enhanced because it is destined, by authoritative authorship, to occur in our lives for *its own purpose,* thereby relieving us of responsibility of human frailty in the conduct of social lives. Heaven, of course, does not "allow such things." We rationalize failure, loss, stupidity, vulnerability, rejection, desperation, destructiveness, etc., with highly fluid (although we perceive them as firm and solid) explanations that "make things fit together" in cause and effect fashion.

Moral Ideology Role #6: Gaps in Reasoning: Every operational "format for effective living" can be "functionally" construed as a maneuverable, stratified, "tentacled," adhesive which exists abstractly *beyond* the *boundaries* of specific concepts which comprise its basic building blocks. These systems articulate a cause and effect chain of events to explain "reality," which ranges from day to day behavior, to global macro-systems of universal ecology. As patterns of life manifest themselves, however, and with our limited intuitive or complete understanding; a dilemma arises. The total picture of rationalistic, positivistic, deductive, and linear existence "progresses" itself through a series of syllogistic assumptions and conclusions to the point that a "dead end" or impasse is reached. Logical reasoning no longer "connects" diametrically opposed, or mutually exclusive-appearing *explanations* of purpose, function and "productive" association between inputs and outcomes of life. Anomalies occur as we assign meaning to perceived discrepancies between coexistence of birth/death, success/failure, war/peace, competition/cooperation, love/hate, independence/dependence, front/back, progression/regression, +1/-1, etc. Even words and thoughts represent "semantic-differentiated" symbols of opposed contradictory/nullifying phenomena. As confusions are precipitated with paradoxes and inconsistent explanations that eventually "consume themselves in their own consumption," we experience psychic anxiety to realize we have run out of answers. This suggests that previous ego-stabilizing "truths" are actually "falsehoods." At this point, life appears an unexplainable journey which all of us undertake, at great expense of valued "commodities" of time, money, energy, hope, attention, worry, etc. The result of nothingness at the end, may parallel the "no-thing" we were, or think we were, at the beginning. As anxiety threatens to become stronger or more chronic, humans individually or in cultures desperately seek overriding explanations. Answers are sought to explain the "unexplainable," or at least validate a "reason" (Destiny) for the existence and persistence of phenomena we do not understand, and cannot rationally explain. Moral ideologies attach emotional-type values to these explanations, which makes the frightening world seem "human," and posits benevolent "chief architects" who produce pleasure rather than pain in the helpless lives of evolving beings. Gods, also, assume responsibility for the full range of actions and attitudes which compose various life journeys. Moral beliefs are "logically right" because they control the "big picture," and are "emotionally right" because of inherent "rightness" that emanates from the "centrality" of their origin in the prime source or universal vortex of creation. In this context, they exist as "untarnished" exemplars of the ultimate essence of reality and the pure strains of relevancy. Morality is correct because it came from the "boss," and also because *it* (the moral principle) says that it is right. This is opposed to other concepts which simply symbolize the "real" without "doubling back" on themselves to also affirm their authoritative nature.

Moral Ideology Role #7: Parental Protection: Religion offers specific and generalized gratuities, protections, guidance inputs, assistance with burdens, and ablutions of presumed or actual wrong doings. These benefits occur relative to a superior, infinite, all-knowing, sympathetic and "interest-invested" creator. Benefits allow humankind regression to "domains" of early childhood recollected security, and/or an equally advantageous opportunity to "counteract" apprehensions, and painful realities which accompany even current existence. Regardless of the actual or fantasized existence of a God-figure, life parades an assemblage of natural disasters, emotional "losses," accidental tragedies, disgusting injustices, and confusing problems before its entire community (at one time or another). This tragic mosaic presents a disorganizing blow to our integration and homeostasis-seeking egos. Tragedies, also, precipitate cognitive insanity (relative to contradictions of formidable events and cultural ideologies about a positive world) without human ability to surrender and find solace in the womb of a protective and "responsible" parental personage. The human need for such services, causes us to fashion the "resolution function" to correspond to the "need-definition" we already possess. Unfortunately, any true nature of an "active, personal, directional, intentional, mediational, responsible, rational, predictable, or conceivable" God, may be ignored in the process of deprivation-ignited *definition* of a higher power. The God we "see" is the capability in ourselves we "do not" see, and is an "objectified" (actually subjectified) reverse image of our non-selves. This is the creation of the other half of life (am-bivalence). This frightens us because when we are not thinking or behaving, our minds perceive the *absence of perception,* which is the total nothingness our self-concepts and symbolizations try to hide through their own existence: (1) if "self" is exclusively validated with concepts my mind has of a "me," and (2) if these ideas do not exist anywhere except in my mind, then (3) when my mind is not directing its attention "to me," is there a "me" that is still there, and (4) if my mind "thinks" at times without anything to focus on, is there only reality when I say there is, and call it something? With the ability of the created to "create" their creator in their minds and culture, there is every reason to believe that this illusioned or "Pseudo God" will be engineered to reflect human deficits rather than strengths. It follows, then, that humans necessarily envision a relationship with God which (1) accents human weakness; (2) traps fearful souls in a dependency-dominated parasitic prison; and (3) perpetuates self-concepts of "weakness" because we would obviously not have a God if we did not desperately need one. The converse, is that a God who supported strengths would ultimately become obsolete when we become strong enough to function independently. This is demonstrated with reductions in certain perceptions of God as adults achieve material competence in modern industrial society (if cowboys build a fort to keep Indians out and hide behind the wall, they ultimately believe the wall proves that the Indians are still there, unless they challenge this belief and negate the validity of a previous presumed necessary action).

Moral Ideology #8: Intensification: There are no definitive explanations of *why*, neurologically, psychologically or spiritually, humans seek stimulation, activity, variability, depth of emotion, perceptual elaboration, cognitive engagement, aerobic poignancy, or concentrative vividness, etc. There *is* an inclination or drive (whether innate or learned) however, toward intensification of life experiences (including the serial interdigitation of stimulus, relaxation, and resolution), which appears to be a "necessary" aspect of what we define as qualitative life. However, (1) as human desire finds itself constricted by logistics of economic and social living, (2) as ecology is destroyed by "productivity," which reduces "natural" resources, and (3) as the mind experiences limitations on its range of perceptual "objects"; the ideological realms of morality, and religion appear extremely "logical journeys" upon which the mind can "feast itself." This can be done without much fear of social disapproval for "spacing out" or "escaping" (from responsibility to production), and with assurance that the "sensations" visited are intrinsically linked to the central core of life. Also, disappointing "conclusions" about the senselessness and implosive alienation and regurgitation of the "anima" inside us, can be reversed by homogenization of the self within the "ultra-self" (within a superordinate domain). Kinetic "electrification" of the "static self" (life force), is boosted by presumed stimulant power reactors and auras of the God-function. Most of us, at one time or another, have overcome inertia or regressive stagnation through integration of our essences with those of "higher powers." In this effort, we "mass the forces" of vivication, with a result of adrenal and cardiovascular excitation, along with conceptualized "hope" of goal attainment. At other times, rites of passage or rituals of significance are translated into the highest realms of "signifying" intensification. Herein, worldly occurrences (with or without bridging functions of a priest/shaman, etc.) are perceived by us, to become something "greater" than their original "less than" nature. The realms of morality and religion, of course, represent infinite reservoirs of power. These forces can be ceremoniously or conceptually harnessed to serve the deficit needs of human interchange with all life obstacles and resistances.

Social Process

Functions which religion and moral ideology perform for society as a whole, certainly include "issues" of individual personalities just discussed, but also involve broader social "needs." Organization structures of the "church," and moral "rules" of living are (1) codified in jurisprudential law, (2) perpetuated by the media, (3) inculcated into family and school socialization, and (4) maintained through cultural rituals. These interpersonal and group collective functions will be discussed separately in this section of the chapter.

1. *Conformity, Conservatism, Predictability*

The convenience of (a) generalized "rules" which guide interactions with one another, and (b) specific "qualities" of attitudes and behaviors which are always "right" and yield "successful" outcomes, are very *comforting*. When moral principles are attached to acts of socioeconomic productivity, cultures assure themselves of "profit-rendering labor," where workers who struggle to master a "resistive" natural environment, work *harder* than their necessarily "minimal" (especially in start-up stages of production, before cost-efficiency and market control take hold) compensations. This "effort" insures minimal remunerative payoffs from corporations, and convinces workers that their labor relates to higher principles of "self-actualization" and "fulfillment." Actions in the name of productivity are pushed "above and beyond duty," when they are psycho-spiritually achieved by symbolizing daily sacrifices and minimal accomplishments, within a set of "ultimate criteria." These criteria elevate the profane to the sacred, and add "metaphorical energies" to the process and outcomes of worldly action. Working beyond compensation levels of production, and deferring gratifications of rest, anxiety reduction, recreation, relations with loved ones, etc.; can be predictably insured by cultures who teach work forces (and support systems—including women and children's roles) that there are direct *parallels* between attitudes on earth, and competitive achievement orientations and sacrifices at higher echelons of existence. This association of earth and heaven functions to (a) justify the suffering of lifetimes of hard work in corporeal life, and (b) give hope of greater rewards at the conclusion of one's productive years.

The stability of family reproductive and work-support systems is also *enhanced* by defining linkages between parents and children, and the overall collective "identity" of collaborative "consciousness," within "natural" Divine Destiny. Supportively, the perpetuation of culture necessitates an organized system of integrating conforming children into "mainstream" activities. Natural and learned sexual "drives," along with cognitive proclivities for creative exploration, constitute strong forces that detract focused energy from "rational" work/rest patterns. Unchecked passion threatens to expand society through liberal reproductive activity far beyond resource and production capabilities to "feed" large numbers of children, and ultimately dependent older adults. The super-imposition of moral mandates and prohibitions focuses attention away from pleasure-seeking desires, which threaten conservative organization of society that seeks to reduce collective anxieties of the *unknown*. Morality insures mutually beneficial interpersonal "responsibility" because the values, functions, rewards, and punishments that engineer "socially conscious" ideas and actions exist within a frame of reference that seems to "know all." This receives *authorization* and energy from deep within our own selves, at the core of life's essence. This essence is interpreted as basic thought and emotion, which is simultaneously a superior God-Force, that miraculously connects inner and external realities into a "functional whole" which helps everyone feel safe and valuable.

Moral ideology directs codes and practices of interpersonal relationships, where social protocol, etiquette, rituals of "approach and avoidance," norms of marriage and committed associations, employee-employer prescriptive attitudes, etc.; save considerable time and effort in otherwise meticulously negotiating each encounter. We control or eliminate "inevitable" anxiety, which represents "learned misinterpretations" of the negative effects our psychic system undergoes when we discover "opposing" viewpoints concerning the worth of our own existence. We protect ourselves when we erroneously hypothesize that "rejection" by others actually exists as an "effect" on *our* systems, and "proves" something negative about the essence of our being. The moral "imprimatur" becomes a conservative "safety net" to prove the "truth" of relationships, ritual compulsions, and historical patterns; and insures social equilibrium and avoidance of the fearful *unknown.* That which we don't know threatens us with feared truths about the following: (a) our continued animal [ape] status, (b) the naturalness of aggressive instincts to ultimately kill and eat one another, (c) the arbitrariness of ecological and physical stimuli upon our organization-seeking personalities, (d) the greatly microscopic boundaries of tautological/ recapitulative thought and action, (e) the possibility of "justice" or "injustice" in the cosmos which may result in punishments equivalent to "hell," and (f) total uselessness of life. Relationships are distractions from the "basest" realities or non-realities of life, and culture establishes "Holy mandates" for participation in complex rituals which insure our vulnerable selves will be nurtured "by law," if not by choice. Focusing attention on the "specifics" of interactions, lessens anxiety which we allow to emerge when "nothing is going on."

2. *The Church*

Formal organizations of Theological/Theosophical/Philosophical structural embodiment of the "God-Essence," including ordained or informal "leadership roles," play a significant part in worldly and celestial affairs, from several perspectives. These functions include the following:

a. validation of spiritual and religious "truth" through interpretation of historical scripture and the "ex cathedratic" proclamation of principles of "sacred" human life;

b. sociopolitical consolidation of constituent roles for disenfranchised "minorities," and infusion of spirited enthusiasm and restitution for the "survivalistic challenges" destined for socially "inferior peoples";

c. "gatekeeping" protectorate of secularized humanism through social advocacy and therapeutic comfortings/stimulations provided by "ministerial shepherds";

d. "narco-pathic opiated" seduction of impressionably dependent idealists and helpless children who "pied piper" their way to support manipulative barons of religious merchandizing;

e. ritualistic sustenance of behavior tradition through ceremonial auspices over rites of passage, crises of development and joys of fulfillment—which affirm the stability of collective consciousness;

f. illustration of human or human/divine conceptual thought and analysis as a testimonial to the inherent value of critical examination of reality;

g. economic influences on world markets engendered by capitalistic investments and political influences of ambitious clerics, church bureaucrats and entrepreneurs;

h. salvaging of musical, literary, artistic and architectural "genius" throughout the ages via threat of "Firmamental Vengeance" to military, revolutionary and tyrannical barbarians trying to capture the "earth's treasure," and ceremonial excitation of "mystical symbolisms" experienced by the "ideologic faithful";

i. soothing human passions, fearful of self-destructive "nihilation" of the emotional "enigma" of human life force, through "sanctification of life," and provision of sanctimonious asylum within "sacro-social" cliques of the chosen;

j. the thankless drudgery of zealous "Damien/Mother Teresaristic" missionary activities to provide medical, educational, cultural, employment, political and religious support to multitudes of Third World sufferers.

In considering "quasi-pseudo-reactive-or-true" church circumstances, it is apparent that some functions are extremely laudable. They should be praised as reflections of the true intentions of a universal supremacy in the world, or certainly as humane exemplars of sensible laws of cooperative living. The earthly structure of theory and behavioral compliance within the church, as God's institution, may be an *accurate* protrusion of the sacred into the profane (or not yet sacred, not yet sacred again). Educated citizenry, however are challenged to examine processes to translate religion into reality, including misinterpretations which distort the true nature and impact of celestial meaning. We might observe ourselves in the process of "seeking," which may distance our true essence from the origin or result of "perfected being" through the created symbolic ego (self). This may be an unnecessary, burdensome step in otherwise direct contact with the creative

Force. In the event, however, that there is *not God,* or we are unlikely to "know" the nature and intent of a universal God-essence, there *are* some "red flags" concerning "church functions." The church may provide destructive influences, or delay the human journey toward realization of its *own* true nature by using social structures which concretize various "essences" of our "needs to believe," and the organization's need to survive. Some cautionary guidelines, therefore, are as follows:

a. The size, "institutional" prestige, power to define access, presence of authoritative leaders, and availability of validational historical documents and tradition, *provide credibility* to the "truth" of "legislated" principles. This may happen regardless of the authenticity of the domain of focused "reality."

b. As churches become larger, bureaucratic systems necessarily increase in conservatism and tactics of repressive control. This may "reframe" or reverse the intents and contents of divine "messages." Spiritual guidelines were instituted by liberal, revolutionary, deviant and very nontraditional charismatic church founders and/or divine "inspirants."

c. Leaders in theocratic institutions may become "trapped" and alienated in predominant roles of (1) sedentary ritualistic "masters of ceremony," (2) organizational "clerk" and maintenance "functionary," (3) pedantic emissary of fixed teachings and "basic" curriculum, or (4) social servant of dependent and/or manipulative clientele using God or the church as an excuse. If this happens, valuable energies to "enliven" and extrapolate theologic or spiritual credos are lost or seriously curtailed.

d. The church's "need" to validate its reason for existence, pressures clergy to "market" spiritual commodities to paying customers. This influences interpretation of benefits in dangerous directions: (1) exaggerations of the value of spiritual "intensifications" and benefits; (2) elaboration of human "need" for services, especially "deficits" of the soul's "adequate" nature; (3) inculcation of dependency through interpersonal obligations within the structure of emotional, but not necessarily spiritual, need-meeting capacities of groups; (4) expansion of the prevalence and complexity of ritualistic rites of passage which "must" be performed by authorized representatives of the hierarchy; or (5) domination of liturgical activities where "meaningful" participation is "negotiated" only through intercessions of various "in loco persona" proxies, and parishioners are "authorized" to participate, to receive full benefits.

e. Religious leaders can become resentful of various dependencies within "inactive" liturgical roles of parishioners, and engendered in "power differential" status of the "flock" as opposed to the "shepherds." Forced deference is an "illusion of adequacy" of the leaders, who, when controlled by the system (which is unavoidable as long as there *is* a system), may express this hostility in direct, or passive fashion toward "spiritual inferiors."

f. Although churches subscribe to divine laws of authority and institutional foundation, they administratively survive within the operating practices of their economic milieu. "Politically-sensitive" modifications of teachings or practice emerge, for fear of socioeconomic retaliation from "offended" community magistrates from whom "patronage" is desired. This reduces "facilitational opportunity" created by the organizational spiritual vehicle, and necessitates regressive redefinition of dogma to reduce conflict within materialistic survival milieus.

g. The social norm for defining and rewarding community leaders includes the expectation of intellectual superiority, economic substantiality, and cultural sophistication (elitism). Church officials associate with, and negotiate need-meeting reciprocity, from members of social classes who are *higher* in status, or equivalent to at least upper-middle-class "standards." This suggests (1) hypocrisy and alienation from the "common" *flock,* (2) differential understanding of standardized spiritual dogma and realities, and (3) inadvertent collusion with social "elites" who prosper at the expense of the poor.

h. The ethos of collective organization and ceremony, together with heightened "sensations" of spiritual/emotional essences within passionate group interactions and dramatized symbolic ceremonies, may give the *illusion* of "more" than is really there when the "party is over." This phenomenon can be creatively engineered by "choreographopathic" entertainers to appear to impressionable people to represent the true nature of God. Constituents may confuse human emotional responses, with actual spiritual demeanors and effects.

Our Responsible Social Behavior

The "true" nature of morality, spirituality, religion, the church, etc. may be a "given," over which the mortal soul or self has little control. Also, these phenomena may be purely psychosocial "constructions" of illusory reality. They may be manipulated to rationalize and integrate an "expectational" and "experiential" world, where few generalizations guide the public at large. In either case, *each of us is responsible* to the rest of us to create a cultural community where:

a. Religion and morality are *always* constructive and growth-producing.

b. A sufficiently liberal milieu exists, where individual interpretations of "correct or delusional" moral/spiritual essences are tolerated and *appreciated*, as either "Divine Providence" or the wonderfulness of being uniquely "human."

c. An intergenerational and multicultural "rainbow" is perceived, where past/present/future spiritual traditions can accent and complement each other. They should create an holistic matrix of meaningful "maturational" psychic impressions relating to all values of life and its ecology.

d. A "rational" world is considered, where concepts of "truth" are not used to pathologically "differentiate" human beings on "assumed" status hierarchies. Truth should be used to *understand* common and special characteristics as the foundation for mutual respect and cooperative (not competitive) living.

e. A socially sensitive world must exist, where moral, religious and spiritual ideologies and behavioral guidelines are utilized *genuinely* to help the alienated/discriminated/disenfranchised/misunderstood "minorities" (and "majorities" of course).

In these contexts, suggestions of spiritually-sensitive thought, attitude and behavior can help us be sensible, compassionate, optimistic and effective in the conduct of moral and religious living:

(#1) Relativity: Irrespective of the "reality" of moral dogma or God's "intentions" (which allow free will or have been programmed "conceptually at conception"), every person's innate and learned "psychology" will necessarily interpret facts or fantasies idiosyncratically. Those interpretations cannot be totally "wrong" if Divine Wisdom gave personkind the equipment to "think" and "decide."

(#2) Phenomenal Truth: Anyone who can "know" the true "essence" of the Divine world or the moral domain, probably already does so. If they are privy to

ultimate knowing, they probably are not pressured to convince "subordinates" of this wisdom. Personkind may never receive unequivocal "confirmation" of pure perception, so appreciation, enjoyment and humility in having the opportunity (not "outcome" necessarily) to explore ultimate reality, should be the bulwark of spiritual and moral motivation.

(#3) Cultural Pragmatism: History reminds us that religion, spirituality and morality have been interpretively expressed within "contextual" frameworks of social "needs" and environment exigencies. "Situational distortions" contaminate the most profound and "holy" dimensions of spiritual or moral traditions. "Truth" and "right-ness/wrong-ness" based on changing social realities, may actually constitute untruth.

(#4) Personal Vulnerability: Psychological defense and adaptation mechanisms in conjunction with childhood dependencies, and "maturational" understanding of ironies and precarious balances of ecologic life, place us in "positions" to create discriminative judgments to exacerbate self-esteem. We inappropriately elevate our worship or obsessively-cherished heroic role models (whom we frequently despise and diminish ultimately), or depreciate the qualities of others, with "ballisticized weapons" of morality and religious condemnation.

(#5) Human Need: Every decision made by humans is an "attempt" at (1) environmental and intrapsychic adaptation, (2) inspirational salvaging of the deepest quality of human energy or life force, (3) defense of the frightened child within, and (4) a progressive effort to achieve an elusive and confusing status of personal worth and usefulness. Despite the horrible consequences of some people's trauma-based efforts to become "one" with their satisfactory self, we all try to be "good" in a *genuinely* human and,

therefore, humanely "perfect" way. Some of us have to be controlled to reduce harm to ourselves and others—but *no one* deserves to be called "bad," or deserves cruelty or death (in legal or illegal ways) because they are people!

(#6) Passivity:

Despite the evangelical spirit demonstrated in many spiritual organizations, the predominant theme and operating pattern of religious bureaucracies is conservatism and *control.* This nudges constituents toward passive and reactionary, rather than assertive and progressive, participation. Whether we subscribe to the "veritable" inspirations of life/faith by an existent God, or feel that spiritual "auras" help us accentuate the self—a vigorous, effervescent, "kinetic-progressive" spiritual practice offers the most hope for freedom, social justice, compassion, and personal growth. Religion must emerge beyond church walls which confine it, and spirituality transcend that which "defines" it.

(#7) Functionalism:

Religious heritages serve identical "functions" for all who subscribe to a human or spiritual universal "dynamic," that may be *obscured* with articulation of specific concepts and ritualistic practices of individual sects. International, intercultural and inter-human *sanity* and spirituality can be best served by emphasizing the *process* of religion first, abstract concepts/principles second, and specific dogmatic and procedural content last.

(#8) Scapegoating:

Religious clergy are socially "ascribed" ineffective roles when we view them as "parental" authority figures who carry responsibility for *our* relationships to *our* Divinities and Gods. They become objects of resentment for the hypocrisies that *we* perpetuate and allow. We venerate their superhuman roles to the extent that they fail (or we will de-elevate their status), and we regress spiritually, with too much effort on expecting *them* to "actualize" the ethos of "God on Earth."

(#9) Manipulation: Many aspects of "tele-vangelism" and modern religious ministries are destructive to psychologically and socially "undernourished" and deprived peoples. The vulnerable expend "fortunes" of energy and money "buying" attention, hope, and enthusiasm for life, which are effectively marketed for target audiences. All are responsible for the continuation of these activities, without some form of quality control. We are even more to blame for tolerance of social conditions and economic depravities which place underprivileged and "hungry" populations "at risk" for manipulative exploitation by sociopathic "God-mongers."

(#10) Freedom: Religion, spirituality and emphasis on qualitative living (morality) are inherently or functionally "good" things to explore, enjoy, and "culturize" for the enhancement of life. *All* spiritual traditions should be freely taught and expressed by children in school, church or other public settings so that everyone can learn from everyone else. *Basic* tactics of "life enhancement" can be acquired and cherished by all. Repression of religion and spiritualism is destructive of the most basic dimension of the human spirit's effort to know itself, its origin, and its destiny.

Chapter VI

THE FUTURE AND HUMAN CREATIVITY

Many spend time cognitively and emotionally running toward a future, because we're escaping a conflict-ridden and hurtful past. We also flee uncertain "anxious" futures by clinging to "illusioned securities" of regressive childhood (which was a "known" commodity). We can benefit, therefore, from projective planning, as "time appears" to move us in presumed directions of anticipation and hypothetical "need." These "movements" and needs include thoughts, behaviors, social adjustments, and cultural problem-solving in time and space "dimensions" which have not yet occurred. These domains escape attention because minds are trained to exist in the "un-" or "completed" realities of past or future.

Personal and social segments of living, represent potential conflicts and anxiety-producing/anxiety-reducing turning points, where we have opportunities, but don't always select *universal human compassion,* and healthy interpersonal or intrapsychic adaptation/growth/mutuality. Positive choices are opposed to past cultural themes of alienation, distrust, paranoia, discrimination, bureaucratized insensitivity, brutal war, destructive competition, and hopeless illusion which have been discussed previously. At impending junctures of future historical life, *every* citizen has a proactive *or* patho-regressive *"decision"* to make. Choices can represent creative actualization of the qualitative "self" expressing its healthy ("natural") human essence, rather than contrived or destructive social definitions of what is "right" or "wrong." Decisions enhance, or detract from a unified and sensibly coherent panorama of enjoyable life for *everyone.* Positive decisions *necessarily* oppose "selective" culturally indexed classes of "haves" and their "have not" counterparts. Humane choices are also contradistinctive to racial, cultural, organizational and personal distancing of "selves" from other equal "selves" in the names of "God, pragmatism, sophistication, productivity, creativity, security," etc. Each of us *must* assume responsibility for the opinion, philosophy, attitude, motivation, value judgment, and behavioral pattern we demonstrate or fail to share, in every issue affecting life. We know in our deepest emotions, there is *really* no way of permanently escaping the following propositions: (1) "Truth" is what we "decide" it is. (2) Culture is not "alive" and, therefore, cannot absolutely control destinies. (3) We cannot ignore massive human suffering. (4) Other cultures are not "inferior" to ours. (5) Material success is not the complete answer. (6) We are all co-conspirators in social hypocrisies which "cancer-ate" us and our children. (7) We are not truly "good" while some others are truly "evil"—and we unequivocally do not "know" the difference. (8) Our illusions of "freedom" from management and "market" control are genuine. (9) One way of "knowing" or "doing" is decidedly not superior to other "frameworks" which exist simultaneously, or have existed previously in history.

Population Control

The world community has lived under the assumption that human reproduction is a "natural" process and "inalienable" right of citizenship, irrespective of consequences to the "personalities" of the "reproduced." Society has virtually ignored cost/benefits to cultures, wherein rates of childbirth are "viewed" as uncorrelated to commensurate systems of economic production, education, social service, health, ecological management, recreation, burial, population control, religious opportunity, etc. As this belief about unrestrained or unplanned pregnancy has expanded, the world has obviously been "plagued" with a vast array and depth of societal *developmental problems.* Additionally, their resolution has been unsuccessfully negotiated along governmentally funded or "privatized" systems of cultural response. In both cases, social and psychological service professionals, who are charged with problem-solving, have never *controlled,* or had substantial access to the following: (1) means of support through economic production; (2) mass media for comprehensive education of society; (3) policy-making components of government for creation of laws and regulations relative to child, adult or family welfare; (4) effective communication with legislators who try to handle the problem via negotiated "deals" between production vs. consumption; (5) medical technology to enhance qualitative "maturational" processes; (6) philosophical belief systems to discuss and explain reproduction as a symbolic as well as bio-instinctual domain of decision-making; (7) formal educational systems to integrate community and family planning topics as part of continuing education, or (8) "noninvolvement" in institutions of cultural life, where "exclusions" of humanistic professionals could, at the very least, *not perpetuate* the problem through ineffective service delivery systems (institutionalized residual "welfare" practices, and "calcification" of middle-class values through "diagnostic" and "pathology-treatment" practices created by "haves" for imposition on "have nots" [if you hold the lid on the "garbage can" you are still part of the "garbage problem"]). Given the above mezzo-level system for "reacting" to overwhelming "child production" problems, plus failures to comprehensively address "causes" of "this many of us," the following *concerns* face a world which ignores unrestrained and symbolized "intercourse"-without-effective-birth-control:

1. There is massive malnutrition and starvation among too many children, adults, and elderly in "Third World" countries. They lack technology, resources, social organization, cultural aspirations, and democratic governmental process to bridge the gap between production and consumption discrepancies.

2. There is substantive maturational underdevelopment, some starvation, and cultural despair, among children and the elderly of *industrial* countries. Large numbers of dependent, nonproducing, and powerless citizenry exist confusingly in "lands of plenty." Their deplorable existence is the result of (a) "intellectual" preoccupation with middle class "entrepreneurial" pursuits, where bureaucratic "mentalities" and organizational structures uphold hypocritical hierarchies of culturally symbolic statuses which accompany techno-industrial success; and (b) perpetuations of anti-mainstream cultures that necessarily survive through self-maintenance and purposeful alienation and victimization.

3. There is unplanned growth (generally) of all families where: (a) "quantities" of children function as "indirect" outcomes of sexual activity for symbolic (intensification, aggression, spiritual transcendence, emotional dependency, erotic control, etc.) or anxiety-reduction purposes; and as (b) direct intentional solutions to questions/fears of relevancy, loneliness, insignificance, "finiteness," "productivity," entertainment, or cognitive challenge.

4. There is large scale alteration and destruction of the "natural" ecology as a result of frequency of use by disproportionate numbers, plus "unsympathetic" exploitation by capitalistic "producers" in underdeveloped countries. Angry disenfranchised or overly indulged citizens in modern industrial countries also represent large numbers of abusers of environment and resources.

5. There is extensive psycho-emotional neglect and abuse of inordinate numbers of children among *poorer classes*. These children's "explorations" and natural behavioral variations become frustrations within family systems already hyper-burdened by stresses of survival within "exclusionary" environments which communicate high aspirational achievement messages. Neglect and abuse among upper-level classes are "defenses" against hypocritical illusionary life values which fail to satisfy sanity-seeking minds.

Cognitive manipulation and control become the only weapons to rationalize alienation of the "well-fed" self, from "itself."

6. There is incredible competition and prestidigitatious manipulation of consumer groups (including defenseless children, a la Saturday morning cartoons + toy/food advertisements which *work*!!) who are large enough to influence market patterns, and represent impersonal assemblages which require little compassionate responsibility or respect.

7. There is lack of appreciation of each unique mind—with multiple minds in many families to deal with—and the mind's vast dimensions of (a) creative, spiritual, emotional, and cognitive potential on conscious, unconscious and metaphysical planes of existence; plus (b) widespread inattention to nuances of emotional feeling, which become "lost in the crowd," when there are crowds.

8. "Standardizations" of economic, spiritual, religious, psychological, social and cultural life, are "genericized" and "mediocritized" stimuli for the masses. Homogenization includes monolithic "apparati" to channel, divert, control, synthesize, systematize, regulate, generalize and otherwise "...ize" the public. Much of what the public experiences has lost distinctiveness, idiographic identity, or specialized uniqueness, in favor of commonly recognized mastercard, golden arches, public ritual, dress "code," automobile, suburban home, etc.

Given implications of the above concerns on the opportunity to exercise one's life in constructive, effervescent and "relevant" ways; our worldwide penchant to rear children with little "strategic" or "tactical" regard for quality of life issues, suggests the following lines of *questioning:*

1. Does anyone *really* derive additional benefit from more than one child, when serious effort is made to explore, understand and enjoy the vast territory of a singular human mind?

2. Is there credence to the concept of security and excitement "in numbers"? Can benefits of multiple human "contacts" be obtained through adjustment or expansion of parental minds and emotions, and through contact "between," rather than "within" family units?

3. Does *any* justifiable rationale *ever* exist for permitting the birth of children in poor families, where most are doomed to lifetimes of hunger, frustration, emotional deprivation, and social "maladjustment"? Also, does "freedom"

include the "right" to subject children to permanent suffering, regardless of child-rearing payoffs to parents?

4. Should mandatory licensure, authorization, and education be extended to "parenting" and family-life agendas? Would massive social efforts to prevent child abuse and neglect (i.e., family stabilization [job training, home repair, police protection, literacy education, medical care, legal services, etc.]) be less costly over time than billions of dollars spent annually on rehabilitation programs which *do not work?* Do planners get "effect" and "cause" mixed up as foci?

5. In cases of religious or moral prohibitions against artificial birth control, are there offsetting "losses" in destructive relationships with unwanted (or prematurely conceived) children? How does this compare to possible "deficits" involved in recreational sex? Where do creative or tension reduction activities *outside* the framework of sexual intercourse fit into this matrix?

6. Does the world community gain anything from *volume* of people relative to ideas, energies, talents, or sheer (unqualified) "presence"? Furthermore, what is the "universal benefit" of continuing human life, at all costs, relative to losses of "non-life," which, of course, would have no qualitative meaning without "life" as its "presumed" antithesis?

7. Would worldwide "humanitarian" gains emerge with international efforts to control indiscriminate human proliferation for a period of limited time? Can we bring production in line proportionately with consumption, but also institute preventive programs to raise the economic and psycho-emotional standard of living for everyone?

Moderated Litigation

Industrial societies have "expanded" the philosophic premises of equality, justice, human dignity, personal privacy and social equilibrium (1) beyond beneficial "functions" as conceptual guidons of the basic *relevance* of human life (2) to insure the inverse significance of personal acquisition, attainment, identity construction, idea building, and personality growth, as inalienable "rights" of "selfhood" to "become more of itself." With layers of social meaning beyond the "original meaning," jurisprudential philosophy and practice now allows any "self" to insult its own dignity and natural expropriational boundary, through "due" processes that involve the following:

1. They reinforce conceptions of human "insufficiency" through ludicrous allowances of "victim" status (therefore litigational opportunity) for *every* facet of living or not living.

2. They perpetrate cognitive "delusionalism" through plaintiff/defendant case presentations based on "winning" rather than the "truth."

3. They allow grossly exorbitant "damage" claims where litigants cannot, in most cases, meaningfully "participate" in the "justice" process. Insurance or business corporations are the only "capable" payees for courtroom "enterprise."

4. They base "decisions" on materialistic or emotional "losses" which are indirectly related to the real issues "at stake," or represent remunerative "gains" that never compensate for "losers'" perception of their "hurt." In fact, they dramatically continue the defendants' retention of dependency on illusions of "missing aspects of the self" (the more money is awarded, the more the injured victim justifies the need, and the inadequacy of material commodities to compensate the "heart").

5. They provide a "legitimate" arena for alienational relationships between people, which distances the self from its dark inner nature (projected onto the contentious opponent) and confirms perceptions of irreconcilable differentiation within the human race.

6. They justify "angry, retributional, and inflictual" formulas for equilibrating psycho-perceptual imbalances of need/esteem, which supports regression to parent-child dependency conflicts. These attitudes affirm irresponsibility (others are responsible and must pay—e.g., "cigarette companies *cause* us to smoke") in living and negotiating life.

Society requires a public system for assigning "guilt" for criminal actions, particularly where incarceration protects the public from irrational and sociopathic intrusions. However, the continued "perpetration" of "anti-perpetration perpetrational" litigious court practice only heightens the "rationality-seeking" individual's pessimism about a compassionate and cooperative world. "Litigationology" plunges an honorable legal and "jurisdictional" profession into greater depths of impudence and discreditable public disappointment and distrust. To moderate the entrepreneurial, sociopathic, farcical and escalating paradoxical nature of the practice of law and litigation, the following axioms are offered:

1. The theory of law should be teaching and maintenance of knowledge/standards concerning the *mental attitude* of fairness, understanding,

appreciation and similarity; plus elucidation of cooperative techniques of negotiation and compromise.

2. Law, as an intermediary "function," can objectify, balance, and equalize psycho-culturally developed beliefs about relative and differential *value.* Law can instrumentally function as a platform upon which, and through whose processes of human acceptance, different selves *share* and jointly learn the origins and various rationales for symbolized "significance." Interchanges relative to conceptual commodities ("phenomenologic abstractions") can be based on the "value of value" itself, rather than exclusively on one value outcome compared to another, irrespective of the "valuers."

3. Law should "win" only when compromise is the end product of controversial interpersonal assertion. Winning should be further qualified relative to the degree to which "litigants" themselves have negotiated the resultant homeostasis.

4. Legal fees, like therapy fees, should be predicated upon, and held constant, relative to process, rather than prorated on outcome.

5. Law should concern itself, theoretically and operationally, with development of societal concepts and procedures concerning *opportunity* and *ability* of citizens to "not need" codified directives and controls on behavior. This suggests a priori institution of laws of liberation rather than restriction, with incremental de-legalization of society with decreasing numbers of repressive mandates, and increasing breadth of fewer rules of "advantage."

6. Citizens should understand reverse logic of current legal practice, whereby the mind loses "more" power of self-sufficiency and wholeness in proportion to the amount of anything it "wins" or "gains" from external sources. "Victimization" with intent to punish others does not fill emotional "holes" of loss, but payment taken from others makes us, like children, dependent on them, which weakens everyone. Gain is really a loss, because we are only what we "are," and never had external "objects" that actually completed "us." We cannot *lose* or gain emotion since it is an abstract concept that was an illusion from the start.

Media

Mass media (television, radio, journalistic newspapers/magazines, books, and audio-recorded tapes and records) which impact our lives, have relinquished a significant role in the education, "sani-tization," revitalization and emancipation of a world trapped within the web of its own dysfunctional system. This is a system of "competitive production, ritualized defense, bureaucratic stabilization, ideologic differentiation, and unidimensional social class progression." The media is a "living organism" that must also "survive" within the hypocritical jaws of a society torn between anger at its own vulnerability, boredom with its daily being, and fear of the colossal "force" which has "apparently" caused its extraordinary existence. In this process, media relegated "responsible" contribution to a problem-filled world, by *adapting three* basic *"attitudes"* toward its operational and philosophic function:

1. Objective *"documentation"* of "descriptive" information, useful in delineating the occurrence, magnitude, and outcome of events, leaves "publics" with different educational, analytic and orientational foci, to their own "devices" (they interpret the "right" way according to socialized views of the "truth"). Citizens should understand *why* events transpired from a multivariate viewpoint, and *how* they could have been enhanced or avoided by employment of alternate beliefs and behaviors among parties involved. Some documentaries, of course, involve thorough investigations and analyses of historical happenings, but these highly qualitative media presentations represent a minority of programs, and are directed at narrowly defined audiences.

2. *Adversarial stimulation* excessively occurs, in accenting inter-human, or person/environment conflict (soap operas) and demonstrating varieties of personal *differences*. This includes exposure of societal "pathology" and heterogeneous conceptual and behavioral "territory" between the "normal" and the "deviant" (Donahue, Oprah Winfrey, Geraldo, etc.). It may not help to confirm the "universal" contradistinction and dissonance between good and evil, and perpetuate illusions of simplistic and polarized causes and effects of complex realities. Also pathological, is the exposure of hero/heroine hypocrisy and human vulnerability in the genre of sensationalistic intrusive moralistic "journalism." These programs seek only to boost economic marketability of "revelational witch-hunts" (Enquirer, Watergate, "Sex" scandals) and avoid opportunities to educate audiences about our own conflicts in human/sacred ambivalence, or teach acceptance and compassion. Serious inquisitions might helpfully "expose" the myth of the "tragic hero," which culture perpetrates with dollars and emotional energies, as avoidance and projection of its own parent-child independence/dependence conflicts. Media might elucidate values of systemic responsibility for all "happenings" in our communities.

3. Senseless "cutsie" *entertainment* or patronization of middle-of-the-road safe values (usually white, conservative, upper-middle class, Western, and

boring) is destructive and uneducative. These programs focus on high Nielson viewer ratings, not offending anyone, and extending comfortable and antithetical "happy face" beliefs about an Alice in Wonderland world. This facade is illusionally reinforced with syrup-coated interchanges between T.V. or radio "personalities"; and subsequent reports of innocuous "community" events which are never discussed honestly, and usually do not represent the "community." Musical recordings and tapes more closely approach "honest" depictions of the fuller range of emotions and life events, although social tragedies seem displaced by exaggerated and/or pseudo-love tragedies. Also, popular music is dismissed by the general populace as (a) "teenage music with discordant loudness, but no message," (b) simply "not my preference," or (c) yet another attempt by liberal factors of society to "mess up" the comfortable status quo.

Given monumental visibility and attitudinal conditioning capability of all media, there are socially responsible "postures" which might create positive and humanly functional changes in society. This can occur without destroying the important role of entertainment and stimulation for all audiences. Suggested media emphases are as follows:

1. Illustrate "causal" psychological and cultural dynamics which "synergize" each other to produce publicly documented events. Elucidate alternate "paths" individuals, organizations or communities could employ to influence results of negative "news," and to resolve conflicts.

2. Emphasize common needs, predicaments, fears, challenges and value orientations which "homogenize" rather than differentiate each of us from each of the rest of us. Elaborate generic "themes" of living, rather than diametric behavior opposites. Media can help humankind merge its creative wisdom and experience to resolve the destructive aspects of humanity interacting with itself holistically, and within specific domains of particularly maladaptive life agendas.

3. Provide analytic presentation of the strengths, capacities, personal attributes and symbolic goals of prominent public figures. This enables the world's hideous pathologies, along with admirable heroic traits, to be integrated into theoretical and pragmatic models of "adaptation," to teach formulas that help people survive or thrive. Provide a forum for the examination of values of cultural life, and help citizens evaluate the "costs" of various adaptational (conforming or deviant) schemes and social viewpoints, as calculated relative to "benefits" for self, others, and society in general.

4. De-emphasize the entertaining capabilities of its own (the media's) identity, and creatively "empower" audiences to be "entertaining," "stimulating," and exciting *themselves*. Media can *precipitate* rather than simply *react to* multiple forms of energetic action and progressive accomplishment.

5. Increase awareness of "real" issues and true conflicts/controversies/value dilemmas involved in human decision-making. This keeps the world honest and humble, and creates truly educated and sophisticated media consumers. Citizens should refuse to be controlled, lied to, manipulated, placated, or otherwise insulted by the world's "magicians," political "money changers," and pathogenic "advertising engineers."

Sexuality (Homo and Hetero)

Sexual activity in the high technology future will certainly be backgrounded by the following: (1) virtual guarantee of 100% effective birth control (for men and women); (2) elimination or effective control of the AIDS virus and extinction of heretofore non-fatal sexually transmitted "diseases"; (3) effective fertilization of the female uterus, and management of embryo growth without disease or other maladaptive influences, including comfortable birthing procedures; (4) approval of homosexual (gay and lesbian) relationships as appropriate and "healthy" environments for "nonnatural" child-rearing; (5) increasing acceptance of gay and lesbian sexual preferences as less "pathologic" and immoral; (6) continuation of prostitution as a secondary "outlet" in either illegal or licensed formats; (7) continued traditional family organizational rearrangement; (8) perpetuated symbolic erotic sexuality in the mass media, the entertainment field, and advertising; (9) expansion of genetic engineering within limited numbers of "family units"; and (10) expansion of inter-social and inter-cultural romantic, sexual, friend, and primary relationship configurations—which means extensive cultural crossbreeding worldwide.

Since the above circumstances are (1) spearheaded by technologic advancement, (2) represent substantial market advantages for techno-medical and health businesses, (3) suggest continued changes in already-revolutionized roles of women and "minorities," (4) corroborate increasing trends in international business corporate mergers, and (5) can be capitalized on by advertising enterprises—there is no way anyone will *halt,* or substantially *delay,* inevitable changes in lifestyles related to sexuality. In fact, efforts to "regress" prior to the conclusion of "natural paths" of sexual innovations or improvement, or attempts to rally defensive (offensive?) or prohibitional blockages in education, social policy, governmental regulation, or religion; will add "fuel to the fire." Ultra conservatism will produce greater resolve among uncommitted citizens (enticed by advertisers who play both sides of the consumer and producer fences) to resist being told what to do regarding "private" sexual values and activities. The logical position for the responsible individual, is a philosophy of respectful and exploratory (educational, not vindictive) "waiting," secondly bolstered by a positivist view of the *functions* rather than *behaviors* of sexuality. We can share awareness and problem-solving suggestions with others, and cooperatively discuss negative results of continuation of past sexual "maladaptations," or emergence of new dimensions. A positivist view, in my "positivist" view, contains the following value positions and pragmatic awarenesses:

1. Psychologic or social "dysfunction" from "erotic" ("sexy, sizzling, manipulative, liberal, passionate, aggressive, uncontrollable," etc.) sexuality, through symbolic images "acted out," relate most to human themes of aggression, control, dependency, self-absorption, unification with a primary nurturer, emotional intensification, and autonomy from external constraints and tension reduction. All of these functions are interchangeably, alternately, or simultaneously expressed via "permission" of uncontrollable (and therefore "un-culpable" and relatively guilt free) physiologic response cycles. This suggests the starting point for understanding and "resolution," is personal cognition and emotional developmental "process," rather than sexuality per se.

2. "Themes" of sexual appearance, seductiveness, attraction, pleasure, etc. are "permanent fixtures" in social life, but routinely are relegated to the "free space" of "nonmarital relationships" (although are allowable by some value positions "within" this context). This necessitates consideration of (a) unnatural or constraining aspects of "marriage" status which inhibit a "natural" or "necessary" attitudinal or behavioral pattern; (b) relatively widespread "need" for multiple sexual expressions which could be accomplished "traditionally," and "programmed" into *normal* adult development; (c) re-emergence or discovery of adult developmental and sexual "needs" which have not been resolved in transitions between earlier stages of growth, and should be addressed relative to continuing deficits on the psychic structure; (d) the manifestation of animal or innate human tendencies in intensified and socially "cosmeticized and dramatized" form, which may be artificially restricted by cultural "domesticizations."

3. Human reproduction as a spiritual and sacred expression of "pure" and deep intimacy has been mitigated by antithetical cultural socialization and conditioning: (a) the act of creation of life must be more effectively attached to each "self's" central "essence," and accented in early socialization of the profound sanctity of the creative self in *all* (not just sexual) aspects of its existence; (b) unconflicted "pleasure" in life is blocked, to the extent that

"recreational sex" has "contaminated" or intermingled with procreative sex, which must be separated by "freeing" the pleasurable expressions so that differentiations between profane and sacred can be evaluated; (c) child reproduction and rearing have lost major aspects of their higher emotional or spiritual significance, and life-creating sexual intercourse has been regressively "diminished"; (d) sexual pleasure, reproductive "consecration," and physical pleasure actually "synthesize" within a more universal domain than culture has "understood," which suggests that differentiations among them are artificial and restrictive of a broader "explication" of the natural order of human expression; (e) many physical and "recreational" pleasures attached to sexual excitation include culturally learned responses which were not intended by universal architectural "powers" to be attached to the reproductive cycle at all; (f) the vulnerable and weak nature of the human mind and will, manifests inability to control sexual pleasure outside the boundaries of reproductive and "primary marital" relationships, and, suggests that culture has applied *artificial labels* to physiologic process to accomplish other functions.

4. Prostitution will always exist, and should be evaluated relative to useful *and* destructive functions, and physically safe vs. unhealthful outcomes. In this regard licensure may help, but will not eliminate the problem, particularly as long as it is considered a "problem." More openness regarding sexuality to de-mystify its aura, will place "it" in a balanced societal perspective and role "repertoire."

5. Technologic reproduction cannot be stopped, and offers tremendous potential to reduce incidence of genetic "inferiority" of diseased and handicapped children. These advances will "program in" adaptive capabilities of humans without anger, aggression, fear and destructive vulnerabilities; and produce general qualitative physical life for everyone. The human race cannot choose or actualize a return to the past, which we do not understand relatively anyway, and the capability of the mind to expand its expertise appears both natural and inevitable. Fears of the elimination of emotion, faith, compassion, etc. are only relevant when considering powers of one faction of humanity versus another. Individuals and cultural conditions can already produce "nonhuman" humans as computers or robots. There may be no comparative criteria to differentiate generations with differing degrees of humanity, except universal law—which none of us can probably know anyway.

6. Although lesbianism and male homosexuality are uncomfortable topics and value positions for many people, we must recognize that alternate lifestyles have *always* existed in *every* culture. "Homosexuality" has been a part of

history ever since history was history, and will probably never be eradicated. In fact, "differentness" is one *constant* factor which has precipitated the great changes, advances, and achievements of every culture. None of us knows the truth and if we did, we would not need to argue or debate it with anyone. Therefore, our best hope of understanding ourselves and others on this issue is to identify and support areas of "common ground" and shared value. Seeing the big picture, we clearly note that gay and lesbian people are trying to love (is this a crime, sin, or mental illness?), want caring relationships like *everyone* else, and try to have courage to stand up for their beliefs. They also want very, very much to be understood and listened to—just like everyone else.

Professionalism

There is little doubt that the world (modern industrial societies), has made a tenacious march toward a theory and practice of progressive competence in "valued" areas of work, social contribution, and performance skills. This has enhanced the quality of goods and services which "advantaged" citizens enjoy (which even trickle down, to our less fortunate brothers and sisters). This process has also encouraged and "standardized," qualitative and quantitative criteria for evaluation of various levels of expertise, which can be called "professional." Concepts and behaviors of professionalism have (1) stimulated "productive" competition within and between professions, as a "checks and balances" system to control negligence, ignorance, malfeasance, and lethargy; (2) enhanced licensure and accreditation protection of consumers; (3) supported improvement in academic, technical and on-the-job training programs; and (4) broadly enforced ethical standards and humanistic values as foundation principles to counteract materialistic thirsts for acquisition/success engendered by entrepreneurial "free" enterprise. Despite "positives" of professional norms and attitudes, however, the world experiences "losses" which serve as "cornerstones" (not with conscious malevolent intent) of the "professional" ethos and cultural framework. Some negatives are these:

1. Professionalism causes increasing and often exorbitant *fees* for services, which create absurd hierarchies of qualitative definitions of "capability" (people are not Gods). Professions reserve delivery of services for the economically advantaged whose "needs" are less pronounced than disadvantaged clientele; and have created an insane system of high cost insurance and "malpractice" litigation. This necessitates development of business corporations of impersonal and bureaucratic demeanor to enable professionals to improve capitalistic success, or maintain "moderated" practices under the protective "wings" of institutional association "rubrics."

2. Professionalism produces generations with *elitist* attitudes and exclusionary practice and general living styles. These are problems to the extent that many "professionals" view themselves, delusionally, as superior to "non-professionals," and have "lost touch" with their own "humble essences." Professionals therefore, are "alienated" in many respects from clients, their own human natures, and objective assessment of delineated roles in broader social systems.

3. There is a problem with increasing "specialization" of human services, where costs soar as customers search "evaluational labyrinths" to find the "right expert." In this mass production genre, society views the person as a "fragmented machine" with specialized parts and operations, to the exclusion of "wholeness," and integration of the self and collective humanity and ecology. "High-tech" specialists are viewed with a set of *divine* expectations for precision and guaranteed "perfection," where experts experience enormous pressure to solve all problems within their circumscribed "area." Customers expect perfect outcomes from a bio-psychologic system that is only "perfect" because of the balance of its capability, absolute vulnerability and relative insufficiency.

4. Professionalism corroborates ideologic myths that suggest *only* professionals have the knowledge and expertise to solve the world's problems. This seduces the rest of us to become irresponsible and dependent in withholding skills and abilities to improve the universal environment. It traps the experts in a world of hypocrisy, fear, illusionary deception, dishonesty, manipulation, exhaustion, etc. as they bravely struggle to do everyone else's job for them. They remain "human" and happy within the "pressure cooker" created by unreasonable expectations incumbent in the "professional" genre, and the countervailing irresponsibilities left to the "nonprofessional."

Responsible roles for citizens, relative to professionalism, are not contained necessarily within a set of "non-" or "anti-"professional postures. They more broadly involve a general attitude that the world will only be "saved" when common people *relate* and *help* and *care* about other *common people*. We must "de-mystify" ideologies and prejudicial judgments which separate "selves from themselves and from other selves," and maintain common sense attitudes about direct paths to enlightenment and problem-solving. Peace, justice, literacy, spirituality, etc. will emerge when the general citizenry regain control of a humane world, from professional "heroes, scapegoats, sacrificial lambs, puppets, and overburdened idealists," trying to single-handedly perform miracles. The rest of us cynically sit around, complain, criticize, admire-then-defeat, abdicate, hide, and unfairly hope for the magical answer from authoritarian parent figures. "We the People," in fact, *all* know very well how to feed the hungry, stop war, end discrimination and hatred, help the elderly, and accomplish other necessary tasks for a truly sane and humane world. We should certainly admire hard work, competence, and dedication of professionals, but refuse to "make them" responsible for the lives (and deaths) each of us must experience fully and completely. We all eventually die and no amount of professionalism can deter anyone from the full path of existence and nonexistence—whatever this is.

Social Sciences

Most professionals representing psychology, social work, sociology, psychiatry, pastoral counseling, psychiatric and community health nursing, guidance and counseling, public administration, human subjects research, education, etc.; have demonstrated valiant effort with admirable compassionate motives to "make a difference" in the world. This effort is particularly gallant, because the world is malignantly infected with contortions of human alienation (from self and others), violence and aggression, physical/emotional neglect and abuse, fear and anxiety, distrust, defensiveness (both individually and collectively), malnutrition and starvation, crime and human disrespect, discrimination, and imminent threat of war. Social service "treatment thrusts" run the gamut from individual, family or group psychotherapy to community organization and social policy analysis/development. All these have been supported by considerable attitudinal and behavioral research concerning developmental effects of psychosocial trauma, and evaluations of rehabilitation. Emphases of amelioration, however, have predominantly been *reactive*. This means, that human scientists have delivered their full range of services *after* "clients" have become "maladjusted, uncomfortable, troubled, traumatized," or otherwise disenfranchised from psychologic and social opportunities for healthy thought and behavior. Ex post facto interventions within private psychotherapy clinics, public mental health services, church and school counseling programs, child or adult welfare agencies, family service centers, psychiatric hospitals or outpatient clinics, drug and alcohol rehabilitation environments, etc.; are extremely *expensive* to consumers and nonconsuming taxpayers. Also, *across-the-board,* they have *not* demonstrated indicators of effectiveness which can be reliably predicted from knowledge or manipulation of "inputs." They do not represent quantifiable differences, among the population at large, relative to "general" social and psychological profiles which occur when *no* reactive interventions are made at all. Additionally, there is strong indication in evaluation literature, that a great danger perpetuates itself through delivery of services within frameworks of bureaucratic, government subsidized (including supports from major "medical" insurance programs), and politically partisaned organizational frameworks. Theorists suggest, in fact, "collusionary" malpractices and negligences of entrepreneurial societally discriminatory human service delivery systems. These employ "social scientists" essentially to "control" volatile and "revolutionarily destructive" lower classes (or maladjusted "deviants" from other class groups) by paternalistically placating their desires for equality and opportunity, with minimal per capita welfare "pay offs." This is enhanced by (1) assigning "management controllers" to administer moderate to minimal human service benefits, (2) "diagnosing" deviant citizens through medical and corresponding psychosocial categories of pathology, (3) maintaining jobs in delivery systems to boost morale and productivity/conformity of the middle working classes, (4) providing psychologic and "growth" oriented counseling as ideologic *illusions* of hope and social acceptance, and (5) philosophically engendering attitudes and definitions of reality which conform to the mainline ethic of the controlling social order.

Regardless of the intended or consequential effects of rehabilitative treatment, there is reason for skepticism about enormous costs of "fixing that which is already broken" for time immemorial. There is also ethical concern over the assumption that it is socially "acceptable" and humanely justified to "expect" every one of us to "come out OK" and to provide a net to catch all those who "choose" not to "succeed." Thirdly, there is concern whether social service employees of the federal government, which is underwritten by business, will honestly and effectively confront real causative factors. Interventions occur while social scientists simultaneously hold jobs that, by policy and program mandate, define "professional" activities, and "patho-conflictual" and dependent roles of "patients or clients," relative to and within the very system which corrects the "problem." The professional success scenario, therefore never addresses basic concerns of "class-ism," sexism, racism, poverty, crime, war, family stress, etc. In fact, surveys of social science professionals reveal that many affirm that their "interventions" have little relevance to "causes" of the problems they struggle to overcome. Most are unable to unequivocally document "success rates" in areas of their endeavor. Although idealistic solutions and "humanistic revolutions" are unrealistic, there are steps all of us can take to bring about change:

1. Human service programs must allocate strategic planning and staff intervention to as many *preventive* philosophies and program efforts as possible. This implies willingness to confront and re-prioritize agency and funder policies, seeking alternate sources of monies not encumbered by federal views and regulations, and creatively defining and operationalizing staff and administrative roles relative to "causes" as opposed to "effects."

2. Training programs in behavioral sciences should require massive renovation of antiquated curricula, to include strategies of intervention and cooperative involvement with the controlling and policy-making domains of the world—

business, media, politics, international finance, military, industry, mass religion, and education.

3. The "professional" world of service delivery *must* be substantially infiltrated by volunteers, consultants, agency board members, and community leaders. Human service should become a *generalized* process of interactions between people of equality, compassion, and common needs. Citizen teams transcend barriers of race, class, gender, education, economic status, etc. Problem-solving is not the responsibility of a small corps of "designated proxy representatives," since *quality life* is the job of "every life that experiences life."

4. Social service "educational" thrusts should seriously "invade" mainstream adult and child learning, and social life, to influence elementary school curriculum, quality living programs in high schools, and continuing education activities for adults in the community. This includes the media and entertainment, and all other realms of social and cultural life.

5. We have researched the "problem" from a psychosocial perspective entirely too much, wherein the "haves" are still defining the "have nots" as "all f____ed up" for a variety of documented developmental and social deprivational reasons. It is time, therefore, to put down the research book and work on problems *we all know about,* concerning (a) psychological traumas of the culture of poverty, (b) self-esteem problems of drug abuse which begins with children in deprivational families, (c) difficulties experienced by children from families which need supports of esteem/jobs/money/opportunity, and (d) the inevitable dilemma of the irresponsibility of childbirth by certain profiled parents who can be clearly defined as abusers, neglectors, etc. We must work with (a) children early in their lives, (b) couples early in their romantic or marital relationships, (c) communities at the grass roots of their culture, and (d) mainstream business and governmental leaders who can make a difference through economic development, job training, financial assistance to families, urban development, and control of excessive births through community-wide programs of support and education.

6. Citizens must *insist* on tax dollars for prevention rather than rehabilitation. This will emanate through interested parties meeting with civic leaders, mailing letters to politicians and corporations, occupying membership on boards of every organization, and encouragement of media to publicize real problems.

7. Everyone must *visit* slums, drug clinics, welfare departments, psychiatric hospitals, juvenile gangs—and find out *why* these fellow humans are so incredibly hurt, frightened, angry, distrustful, alienated, depressed, insane, helpless, etc.—*It's not their fault*—it's our fault!

Death

The future will change the physical quality and quantity of that "transitional experience" we value and call life, and the very definition of its meaning relative to changing aspects of its own nature. This includes core values and experiences "during" and after the "dying" phenomenon, as the concluding phase of the developmental continuum of existence. There are tragic consequences and interminable influences of environmental, meteorologic, endo-physiologic, and psycho-neurologic "toxicities" which contaminate the life "syncromesh" which humans insist on "artificializing." Technology and increasing awarenesses of the entrapment of personkind within its own self-made tomb, can produce internal and external "sensitivities" and resolutions of major health "infringements" and illnesses within the near future. This is true for the world's middle and upper classes, initially, who pay the bill. Recent evolutionary outcomes of ultra-sophisticated medical diagnostic and treatment regimens, along with advances in genetic and chemical engineering, will also reduce (unless nature, God, the cosmos, or human "intention" represent intervening variables) the severity of developmental and genetic disabilities. Advances will impact childhood mortality, while simultaneously increasing the longevity of healthy and functional old age (which won't be "old" any more with removal of maturational "deficits"). In this trend, (1) more children will be capable of healthy birth and infant survival, and will be free of "inherited" genetic, "anomalies"; (2) adults will be healthier throughout middle adult years (also due to human "replacement parts"; (3) old age will be entered with a healthier history; (4) the calendrical point of death-relative-to-birth will be extended with effective anti-pathology drugs and laser surgical interventions; and (5) the overall environment will have less pollution and "poison." The body's adaptation to its milieu, and nutritional advances, will further the cause of "health" as an inside agent to transform cellular structure and function to a more efficient and productive system of interaction with the entire life system. Most of us who will benefit from these advances, will not complain about the positive results engendered for the immediate and longitudinal life process. There will come a time, quite soon, however when serious controversy will erupt concerning the point at which mechanically "enhanced" physiology will demand redefinition of "human"-vs.-"machine." This implies substantive debate over the relationship between natural thought and feeling process, and "unnatural" stimuli from ancillary replacement components, which influence the quality of the basic and fundamental "life essence." This issue was somewhat put to rest with the LSD and "mind-altering substance" concerns of the Western World in the '60s, where creditable thinkers and experimenters lined up on both sides of the argument to advocate for the principle of enhanced "qualitative" life. Each revolutionary advocated one viewpoint, while debunking the opponent's position with allegations of "defensiveness" and "protective perceptual isolationism" for refusal to "live" life "fully."

These concerns, as can be expected, will incrementally spillover (and become reactivated) into similar questions about the "end" result of life, as noted in the following issue summarization:

(Q-1): Does prolongation of life in any format, or with certain categories of artificial apparatus, *violate,* retroactively or proactively, primary essence of "humanity" ("personal essence, life force, soul, mental autonomy or destiny, feeling, natural integration with universal environment," etc.)? Also, are any "qualitative gains" perceivable with increasingly unencumbered "quantity" of longevity?

(Q-2): Is the human body sacrosanct to the extent that intrusions into its natural systemic process, offend and "significantly" interdict the blueprinted design of life? Are detrimental effects discoverable as a result of artificial manipulations of "nature"?

(Q-3): Does delay of the fairly consistent and demographically "patterned" death sequence of cellular and energy "cessation," actually postpone a necessary new starting point for "life after life"? Are there other "startings or endings" that represent a comprehensive matrix of universal interrelated "enablings," which we do not see or experience when defining life and death within current rubrics?

(Q-4): Is there anything to be gained by participants or observers of the death phenomenon, through associated cultural rituals of transition to the future "condition" of "being," processes of "closure," receipt of "benefits," or "transcendence"? Do these benefits become violated or mitigated if normal suffering, loss, decline, or sequential "timeliness" are altered to small or large extents by artificial technology?

(Q-5): Is there a realistic potential of creating permanent human life forms, and would this "capability" allow "machines" to really replace "lives"? Is there any "knowable" loss, if nonexistent life (those of us who don't "get born") does not like its replacement "automatons," and what alienations or anxieties will be experienced by the generation who has to live through the actual person-to-machine transition?

Although each question represents a domain of reality which may never be definitively understood—there are "positional" perspectives which responsible future "diers" might consider, relative to the debate which will exacerbate as the techno-"sufficient" future draws nearer. These are represented as "answers" to the "meaning of death" question:

(A-1): Every person has the opportunity, "responsibility," and "necessity," of making their own decision about the meaning of life and death. This decision has *no relationship directly* to similar or different definitions applied by culture. In this sense, how others view this phenomenon (with or without the impetus of technological stimuli), or might actually alter its dimensions, does not necessarily force anyone to acquiesce, unless they are born or mandated to utilize "artificial intelligence." In this case they (or we) will be programmed to experience no conflict. If we are human, we can "be" human; if we are machine, "human" will be unknowable and therefore irrelevant, and we won't know it's irrelevant.

(A-2): We must be careful in distinguishing the "death" and "life" phenomena. "Presumptions, hypotheses, attitudes, and emotions" relative to future death or concurrent death we observe in someone else, may only be "valid" existentially, as representing our *own* interactions with the life experience. This is true even though "death" may constitute the precipitating stimulus for our thought, or may represent the content of ideation. It may be phenomenologically true that death can only be known by the dying, who may also be equally distanced or illusioned from their own "terminal event." This implies (1) "death" dismissed by the living may never really be death, (2) "life" is the only context from which the living can know anything, (3) living people have no authorization to relate to death on behalf of the dying (which ironically is all of us), (4) transcendences across domains (life to death conceptions), across time frames (present to future), and across beings, reduces attempts at reconcilable logic and effective decisioning, or (5) life cannot be understood or known retroflectively from a "position" (point of view of the dying who may only be able to die rather than live).

(A-3): Qualitative attributes of life or death may be illusions of that which will never exist or cease to exist, so ideologic discussions of either one may be irrelevant.

(A-4): Choices about the span of life, the time or cause of death, and the holistic atmosphere within which life leaves the physical (cognitive and emotional) corpus, can be "influenced" by input from everyone, anytime *during life*. Social prohibitions, however (moral, social policies) can force outcome results (artificial life support systems, forced pregnancies among fearful or uninterested "mothers," illegality of suicide, or capital punishment) that ignore or transcend the intents and "free will" choices of those interacting with "death circumstances." These social values and occurrences, most probably, violate their own principles as follows:

1. Life which remains, but is unperceived by the "liver," cannot be valued or appreciated, and therefore appears to lack quality. It may, however, be valued by a superior power but unnecessarily so, because this power values life by its very creation. Also, it probably does not need specific cases to prove any point of view (e.g., artificial life supports when mental life and brain activity have "theoretically" died).

2. Life initiated against the will of otherwise responsible caretakers (prohibited abortions) will, necessarily, be unappreciated, and most likely abused or neglected life, representing *deficit* rather than *asset* for all concerned parties.

3. Life sustained against the will of the adult possessor of already "depreciated life" will perpetuate pain and misery which (a) if intended by the "creator" should not be violated by logically extensive self-annihilation; (b) if needed by the creator will be continued after physical life has ended; (c) if not intended by the creator, then it is an indicator of non-life—as "non-qualitative" life that would already have been reversed, if this were possible; (d) if the responsibility of the possessor of life, has already been decided; or, (e) if the responsibility of others in the environment, cannot be addressed directly by current methods of diagnosing, confining and treating the pathological patient.

4. Life taken against the will of the "apparent owner" will teach no lesson to that life which, in the teaching process, is removed as a "learner." If serious criminals could learn responsible social behavior from aversive stimuli, they would have already done so in connection with the aversive life situations which produced them.

(A-5): Emphasis on death as a "significant" or "loss" experience may cause destructive and exaggeratedly forced "clingings" to life, based on fear and expected "depreciation." The "death" of current meaningful life replaces the death of subsequent life. Society may redefine death as birth (or rebirth, or extended life), partly because life has not been lived as *itself,* because of excessive concern with its eventual absence. Therefore, the absence is where we live in anticipation of the life which has already passed us by. When, of course, we get to "the end," we look back and, again, do not exist in the present. This suggests that personkind cannot tolerate any "now," and always lives in some "not now" which can be controlled and structured to meet presumed need deficits. Even death may be conceived as something related to yesterday or tomorrow.

(A-6): Future efforts to emphasize positive aspects of death (or life for that matter) and encourage meaningful "living through" or "growth" maturation for those dying and those losing a significant relationship, will benefit everyone. This de-traumatizes a natural aspect of life (e.g., its transition, change, modification, return to "negative" existence), and emphasizes the utter simplicity of both the beginning and ending dimensions of existence. This (1) illustrates the futility of neurotic worry about interim phases of that which returns to possible nothingness, (2) calls attention to ideologic frameworks used to redefine life or non-life which was possibly never definable in the first place, and (3) suggests that the worst death of all is the anguish of meaninglessness.

Fine Arts

Creative expressions of relevancies and dimensions of meaning are extremely *neglected* and *underdeveloped aspects of culture as a whole*. This includes literature, music, painting, sculpture, thespian performances, singing, creative design, dance, crafts, and other forms of stylistic, symbolic, abstract-communicational, emotional intensifying or soothing activity. Furthermore, these endeavors require greater development as technology and service functions of ultra-industrial societies create decreasing "need" for basic subsistence, and provide "opportunities" for fuller expressions of "qualitative humanity." The world desperately needs creative ways to share feeling and expand creative potential to reflect the self, as well as positive capacities of interpersonal relationships. It is unhealthy to differentiate and discriminate within the extremely limiting frameworks of language, socialized mental concepts, and cultural ideologies. The fine arts are a necessary vehicle to carry each human "soul" to its deepest amplitude, profundity, primacy, value, grandeur, etc. Arts function as the most culturally nonspecific and non-alienational form of communication and expression by which everyone can "talk and listen." This process universally appreciates the "act of articulation," rather than the *content* of what is or is not said. Just like life, however, the "good things" rarely "seep down" to lower-class gutters or destinies, and fine arts are often used as "discriminatory credentials" to elevate one set of identities above another. Discriminative exclusion, of course, imposes a "maximum benefit ceiling" on the creative journey's path, which further destroys the will to hope, dream and create; and produces generation after generation of unstimulated and unstimulating carcasses of empty personalities. Creativity highlights individuals and groups who *experience* what we don't experience, *accept* what we leave behind, *hurt* where we have no pain, love what we ignore, and *see* "us" from the other side where we do not see ourselves.

From this viewpoint, we should encourage widespread teaching, support, acceptance and sharing of all styles and types of artistic expression from every human perspective. Creative use of mind and talent will influence all other problem-solving domains of social life. It will (1) focus attention on the "waves" of "integration and association" rather than the uni-focal fear of the vulnerable self; (2) encourage utilization of all spheres of "awareness" and energy; (3) activate meanings that exist beyond the realms of simplistic or confining codes of words and culture-specific thought; and, (4) constitute socially unifying and "neutral" focal centers which can be appreciated freely, to avoid defensive and self-confirming "units of conception."

Money

Anti-materialism articulates a resounding need for compassion, "clarity," emotional sensitivity, or communal revolution, to reject the impersonal capitalistic "order" which "seems" to make the world "go-round." Our relationships to the symbolism and physical/fiscal outcomes of the world monetary exchange system would be the initial point of focus. Following—is critique of the material advantages which do *not* accrue to disenfranchised "lower" social classes as a result of selfish ego and socio-centrism of the world's "haves." This includes a reminder to the quality-of-life-seeking citizen, that "money does not buy happiness," nor substitute for other emotional values which its "energy," in fact, often obscures. The "slap-on-the-hand" approach to affluent "monitarians" gets little result, except to create twinges of guilt, which are rectified with acute donations to favorite charities, or moments of kindness to some suffering soul in the "nether world." Nothing, however, would really change because most of us have no intention of "giving" much to (1) help the poor; (2) use ourselves as exemplary sacrificial lambs (hunger strikes, protesting, etc.); (3) become social scientists and "pied pipers" of the suffering masses; or (4) become mystics, priests, nuns, and monks; sequestered in monastic retreats forever to cleanse ourselves and meditate/pray for a pathologic world. What is more useful is for everyone to *examine* roles *we* assign monetary phenomena (and other material commodities, artifacts or ideologic concepts) in our lives. We can further evaluate the extents to which various symbolisms and materialistic rituals have masked or replaced more precious or functional "connections" to our emotional or spiritual natures. First, some philosophic points of view:

1. Money is a transferable token to represent economic and cultural "energy" (value relative to survival, production, consumption, etc.) of a society. It symbolizes "permanency" of its natural resources, systems of production, consumer dependability, increasing aestheticism to expand markets, and organizational and value stability. Current future, therefore, demands everyone's effort to develop (a) resources (natural, service and aesthetic), (b) continued growth of production, and (c) monetary movement to represent active consumerism.

2. The fact that some people or organizations have considerably more money than others is *not* the main problem. Business profits, invested in banking (stable monetary reserve and lending foundation), production, and expenditures of the wealthy, are presently very functional. They provide monetary energy (people work in hopes of obtaining a future idealistic benefit which can be bought with money, or attributed through "appreciation" and pleasure of "authorities") and employment opportunities with the products consumed by the "rich and famous."

3. Money, as a materialistic "exchange" medium, and symbol of "quantifiable" differentiation, represents a basic *concept of human quality* (particularly in Western thought). Rather than suggesting the exclusion of "money's meaning" from our lives, we can appreciate its role in "signaling" the underlying presence of a mystical, esoteric, spiritual, and emotional component of "being" (human). In this regard, we can use money as a "springboard" to even greater interaction with the inexorable richness of the "self," which might be more clearly revealed if we had a higher layer of symbolism called "mega-money" or "ultra-bucks," etc.

4. Material possessions are also *not* the big problem. The human mind is so vastly complex and voracious in its culturally-reinforced quest for intensity and stimulative differentiation, that it requires "grounded reference points" to organize and relax its search (which is a search for its "non-searching" center). "Objectification" stimulates the mind to greater degrees of appreciation, through admiration of its own reflected "eminence" in an external symbol. The configurations of the object nature intrigue our mental and emotional capacities to extend ourselves beyond that which we have created. This is positive as long as the "creator" rather than the "created" or the "process," remains the developmental intent.

5. *The problem*, then, relates to the *use* of money as a behavioral representation of human intent, value, and relevance, and the *degree* to which money (or any external symbolic representation) becomes an exaggerated

obscurational position vis-a-vis the life phenomenon that it represents. Specifics of these problem foci are as follows:

(a) Money should be used by those who have it, to invest predominantly in human "products and commodities." Herein, benefits from "possession" and creative development of value, are balanced between physical objects we enjoy, and other people we help develop. These individuals "pay back" the benefit (as a quality painting or piece of furniture would in our homes) by expressing their "freed up" creativity, when physical survival is insured.

(b) Money can be lost between the cracks in organizations and ritualized systems, or spent redundantly or inefficiently in product or system maintenance with few "developmental or maturational" payoffs. It should, conversely be salvaged and reinvested more fruitfully to enhance "top of the line" products, and people. It can also rescue "bottom layer" products or people who will contribute reciprocally later on. Money "in the middle," however, only perpetuates defensive and trapped bureaucratic processes, and should be extracted and used strategically to get greater energy from its inherent power.

(c) Money should not be given away without reasonable and humane reciprocal expectation of work. Welfare systems should require public or industry "service," to receive basic benefits, with no penalties for exceeding basic subsistence ceilings. Money invested will accrue "interest" in the long run, with (1) enhanced self-esteem of working people, (2) more consumer activity to stimulate markets, (3) development of aesthetic interests to replace criminal aggression or passivity, etc.

(d) Money only represents *inner* human energy, motivation, intent, will, aspiration, value, quantity, etc. We can effectively use money's "representational energy" to remind us of the depth, complexity, and relevance of the inner differentiations and dimensions we possess. We should spend money, but more importantly, "spend ourselves" to achieve the fullest extent of whatever "this" is that we call "life."

Discrimination

Discrimination is the process of formulating qualitative human value decisions about the "worth" and "significance" of individuals singly, or relative to group membership. Also included is differentiated access to social and behavioral opportunities, based on human attributes of color, cultural heritage, gender, physical appearance, previous or current life experiences, economic status, adult age (a broad interpretation of this problem also concerns civil rights of children) or any other "status" or "condition of being." These conditions, categorically exclude understanding of additional, rather than unitary, dimensions or characteristics of the multifaceted human personality. Pronounced forms of discrimination, obviously, decrease or eliminate acceptance of the full range of capacities of "minorities," and ascribe inferior status whereby they receive lesser social rewards for equivalent (or even superior) "performance" to "majority" groups. "Inferiors" are treated in humiliating and degrading ways, causing substantial problems with esteem, anger, decision-making, autonomy, healthy dependency, relationship formation (especially with "majority" persons), civic responsibility and community participation, physical health, economic survival, and spiritual/ religious formation (disenfranchised "victims" excessively utilize unhealthy forms of spiritual salvation, to escape from inordinate pains of discriminatory social life).

The causes of discrimination are clear, regarding relationships between "different" persons and subgroups in society. Discrimination is undergirded by the following:

1. fear of differentness and lack of "value" experienced by everyone as a "general principle" of human vulnerability—

2. "needs" to exaggerate one's (or a group's) belief in their own esteem, through the culturally taught process of competition, aggression, and "winning"—

3. quests for stimulation of anxiety, and the act of establishing discrepancies between at least two "statuses of being" (e.g., present and future expected self, or between one person and another), to handle the dependency of childhood (reactivated in "adult" life) and avoid the experience of nothingness—

4. externalized projections of disappointments (again reactivated from childhood) in the self's insufficiency, which are more safely viewed as belonging to someone else—

5. fear of physical destruction or non-survival as a competitive member of the animal kingdom—

6. expression of the overall significance of human life, used "hierarchically" to validate psychosocial "accomplishments" relative to those who are *not* the "believers, doers, followers, succeeders," etc., and to energize effort to "become" more "fully human," by defining others in "less than" statuses.

Discrimination is *destructive* to everyone, for obvious reasons to those who are the "have nots" and may never be a "have"; but also to the "discriminator," because of the following:

1. There is valuable time wasted on deciding about something over which we have no control and from which, as a result of our actions, we will not benefit.

2. Defensiveness and/or aggressive energy is necessary to deal with retaliations (direct or passive) which inevitably erupt, when the human "spirit" is repressed hard enough and long enough.

3. There is "retrograde creativity" used to articulate *differences,* and subsequently make oneself actually believe they are true or *really* matter.

4. Discriminators lose self-esteem that unconsciously develops when anyone degrades a component of life which they also share. Criticism of the self (even if projected to external selves) is destruction of the self and the value of its ecology.

5. We lose contributions which discriminated parties might have made, to enhance our own self-esteem and provide team support for many struggles and journeys with which we all need help.

6. Conceptual capability is sacrificed, and mind-training is lost, in using brilliant mental machines to simplistically "judge the obvious," and refuse to use human differentness as a challenge to think comprehensively about life's "consistencies" and "inconsistencies." We learn something new from every interpersonal encounter.

7. There are secondary and more generalized disadvantages to everyone who (a) financially supports "cultures" of poverty, (b) prepares defenses against criminals striking back at a system which entices yet excludes them, (c) experiences the "eyesores" of dilapidated neighborhoods and unsightly vandalisms which ruin the beauty that middle-class money purchased at a great cost, and (d) is humiliated by "affirmative action" mandates and other "equality" laws which help to a moderate degree, but destroy freedom for

everyone who is controlled by social policy, hypocritical community expectations, and legal authority.

Regarding the above, there are simple principles which make life substantially better and more autonomous for everyone:

1. Judgment of any kind is "reductionistic" and imposes limitations on both the "judger" and the "judgee."

2. Those excluded from any aspects of life do not go away, and negative energy has a reverberational and retroflective impact on everyone, sometime, within the system.

3. Criteria to discriminate are either physical behaviors, physical appearance, or physical ideas which actually mean very little, or nothing, to those who are not the owners of those characteristics.

4. Discriminations are cognitive and behavior exercises that never have positive outcomes, inside creative minds and emotions which produce them.

5. Discrimination, as a value judgment about a life that none of us authored, is a denial of that life we all live, and a distortion of "real realities" which exist.

6. Society has always grown from differentiation—never from "sameness."

7. No one has theologic, naturalistic, universal, or ultimate authority to "define" a reality we only borrow or share, but never own—this is a law of nature and human transcendence.

8. Precious time is lost in denying creative participation to anyone who can help make all of "this" better.

9. Social "power" and "privilege" to define and judge others is predicated on an extremely insubstantial and weak base of economics, physical strength, social position, etc. "Advantage" always is removed from every soul sometime during the life process—the results of judgments based on weak foundations are generally equally irrelevant. We gain *nothing* when *nothing* is our point, and our authority is based on *nothing,* which is something we all have for only a brief time in time, and then may ultimately have forever.

Technology

Many humanistic advocates suggest that "technology," as an extension of the industrial revolution's "machine age," represents the ugly Scylla and Charybdis mythological monsters which destroy the "human" and "psycho-emotional" foundations of life. These foundations extend into, and philosophically guide, the operational (jobs, organizational structure, public works, community services, recreation, family life, etc.) as well as spiritual components of life. The acquisition of techno-mechanical and "computer mentalities" among children is also hoisted as a flagged skull and crossbones, to apprehensively signal the demise of family (vs. business) influence in life, and the progressive deterioration of "basic values."

Despite various rationales of protestation about the ill effects of techno-mechanistic orientations, and "valuations"; technology has, of course, helped create and sustain the incredible quality of material and psychosocial "life" which is enjoyed, to some degree, by every world inhabitant. Technology will certainly build upon "itself" maturationally to anchor the industrial and service components of an interdependent and expanding world community. This is a benefit we must appreciate, in a world experiencing (1) limitations on natural resources, (2) cost deficits in competitive production "efficiencies," (3) ecological challenges to health and organized/qualitative community living, and (4) health problems which can only be resolved on a large scale through technologic innovation and contribution. In this regard, technology is neither "bad," nor "the problem." It becomes troublesome to many when its utilization procedures exemplify "impersonal" and socially irresponsible/compassion-less attitudes which emerge when people deal with their own inner selves—and "project" this conflict into the material world. Technology becomes dangerous when human dependency needs cause us to allow machines, or more correctly, bureaucratic systems that employ machines for "efficiency and effectiveness," to control autonomous lives. Solutions to the technologic "Jaws" phenomenon, therefore, involve reiteration of common sense and basically "human" philosophic and pragmatic principles. These help align specific components of the "living" process, with other aspects of existence. "Operational" mechanics of daily activity then fall into their proper, or at least "not improper" place:

Remember that . . .

1. Machines are programmed to be consistent and rational and, if not broken, cannot be otherwise (at current stages of computer "reasoning"). Frustrations at them are related to *our* "disorganized" or "idiosyncratic" formulas of the world, which are egocentric and self-serving "rationales" for our own behavior.

2. We use machines to save time and energy. This signals, from a "naturalistic" point of view, that other components of our systems are "out of control" and will remain so, as long as machines and technologies "rescue," rather than guide "decisions."

3. Humans have a wide range of choices, which most of us "choose" not to perceive at all (this takes away *excuses* for irresponsibility and *defenses* against fears of "nothingness," [p.s.—if "nothingness" is actually true, then fears have never actually existed, and fear-related suffering is an illusion of "somethingness"]). One choice we have is how we "deal with technology" as *secondary* to human autonomy.

4. "Technological" thought and content may *actually* be no different phenomenologically from humanistic patterns and contents. Cultural or personal values that elevate one paradigm or the other may be entirely arbitrary—substantively the process and outcomes may be no different.

5. Impersonality that "appears" to accompany "mechanistic" forms of thought and reasoning has several causes, not directly wedded to the technology itself:

   (a) lack of autonomy and creativity in jobs and role performance options of those who use the "techno-assistants";

   (b) unreasonable demands of "customers" who receive services through technologic means of delivery, wanting "perfection" from systems to "make up" for their negatively viewed disappointments with the "perfectness" of parents (recollected from the past) and self;

   (c) exaggerated fears and defenses (incorrectly viewed as offenses) against "competition for survival," which are expressed in unreasonable efforts to streamline all social and organizational operations;

   (d) continuation of compulsive rituals of social behavior which "mesmerize" participants into unthinking stimulus-response patterns that provide secure predictability and satisfy unconscious needs for "purpose" in life;

   (e) resentment of "logic" used elsewhere in evaluating life, where technologies become scapegoats to "carry away" various "truths" of living which destroy the "truths" of living, but which also represent concrete objects toward which anger at ourselves (and formerly at parents) can be expressed externally;

(f) decline in expression of philosophies and "dreams" about life by adults who realized they expressed the "wrong ones" in the past and gained nothing, and by younger cohorts surviving economically in a frightening world, therefore leading to material functionalism.

Organizational Systems

"Systems" are absolutely essential to—(1) "process" functions of production and service; (2) collect, store, and analyze information relative to "effectiveness"; (3) organize interdependent "roles" into collaborational matrices of relevant association; (4) reward useful contributions by participants; and (5) manage contractual relationships between consumers/constituents and service providers. It just won't work any other way, with decreasing resources and increasing/large numbers of people. Unfortunately, most of us become unnecessarily overwhelmed, frightened, dependent upon, and hoodwinked by the massiveness and complexity of "perceptively" impersonal bureaucratic conglomerates. We permit ourselves to be controlled, defined, mistreated, discriminated against, lied to, manipulated, insulted by, patronized, paternalized, cheated, assaulted, lost within, and otherwise dehumanized—by a phenomenon we cease to understand or control for our own best interests. The "losers" cannot "buy" or "think" their ways out of the "octopusian" structure of bureaucratic organization which we all tolerate. Systems, therefore:

1. cause us to forget that, without ritualized goals and objectives in life, there may be no point to all of "this";

2. provide a source of displaced aggression so we don't become angry with our "real parents," or ourselves, for human vulnerabilities we delusionally think should be perfections;

3. control disenfranchised peers whose anger and potential revolutionary destructiveness we mitigate within de-energizing systems;

4. provide organized patterns of relationship so we don't have to evaluate our own acceptability and value to others (value and relevance are, therefore, attached automatically to social and organizational roles); and,

5. generate stimuli to entice production to keep producing, and to support hierarchies of cultural aesthetics to generate social perceptions of "unmet need," which is the space filled by "profit-after-need-satisfaction."

The problem with organization and bureaucratic systems, however, is really a problem with human relinquishment of *individual* responsibility for behaving in rational, sensible, and human ways. We don't deal with a "child" *we* have created, and have decided to scapegoat and allow free reign to irritate and manage our lives. Responsible behaviors, therefore, which everyone can demonstrate in internal or external "connections" with organizations, are outlined as follows:

Responsible Behaviors Relative to Organizations

RBRO-1: Remember that organizational systems have no animated life of their own, and are composed of "individual human decisions" which exist as changeable "units of reality" if we, the challengers, find the "responsible decisioner."

RBRO-2: Organizations will ignore or "hurt" members and customers as long as everyone refuses to "stop playing the game." This is a conservative pattern to avoid rejection and extraction from the system, although greater rejection comes from meaningless collusion. Rejection causes no real loss because we attach ourselves to another system as soon as possible, and continue the pattern.

RBRO-3: Organizations waste every kind of resource, because we attribute "benevolent parental characteristics" to this illusioned control device. We unconsciously accept unreasonable gifts, while resenting our dependence on a "self" which does not really "know" (become one again) us—we must stop needing parents!

RBRO-4: Organizations change by simultaneous pressure from inside and outside, which begins when citizens voice displeasure and refusal to accept conditions as they "are" and "have been." We must assume responsibility to make improvements. Refusal to work to improve one organization means we will be trapped in another one we have also abandoned.

RBRO-5: Organizational systems get out of control and perform destructive behaviors (e.g., Nazi Germany) and, therefore, must be challenged at all phases of their development and operation. This is true even when things are going "good." When they get horrible, it is too late to salvage or correct "logical" system outcomes.

RBRO-6: Change is possible, to some degree, at every location and juncture within every organization. Everyone must do something *every* day to make positive changes—which will always have *some* impact.

RBRO-7: Organizations can be viewed as creative works of art and as synchronized symphonies of spiritual, emotional and human "enablement." This view presents a challenge to free and inspired thinkers to create masterpieces of streamlined and humane effectiveness, efficiency and beauty. We can enliven daily work roles, and provide relevant services and "attentions" to everyone who relies on organizational frameworks (which really means people relying on other people) to fulfill valuable and useful life journeys.

Outer Space

Although major industrial countries have been intermittently or moderately involved in the "space race" for the past 25-30 years, there are numerous reasons to predict massive worldwide involvement in this endeavor in the relatively near future:

1. Current world environment is virtually out of untapped forms of natural resources, and must explore the farthest dimensions of interplanetary environments. This is essential to harness other types of energy and "value" sources, to maintain the machinery of productivity at a high level of stimulation, involvement, and motivation.

2. The world is rapidly running out of space for a population that refuses to (a) share international thoughts strategically, (b) understand population growth dilemmas and (c) control birth or life longevity rates. These problems produce large numbers of dependent persons who typically do not contribute to the productive potential of socioeconomics. We need more property until we reproduce less of us.

3. Great exploratory spirits of the world have conquered most virgin territories and natural obstacles, and grow restless with few escape, fantasy, enchantment, intrigue, domination, or self-actualization "horizons" left to pursue. "Out there" is another New World, and personkind's incessant search for its origins and destiny will push us energetically toward the vast "unknowns" that remain.

4. World economic and industrial communities are beginning a series of international mergers and cooperative enterprises which will ultimately reduce vast competitions that existed as a result of industrial revolutions. This will streamline production, marketing, and distribution, where corporate production will have a good deal of time on its hands. Vast wealth will be centralized in a minimal number of multinational enterprises, which produce the phenomenal capital needed to finance comprehensive space exploration.

Business, not government, will lead the way. Space will necessarily emerge as the new marketplace.

5. Various world cultures have exhausted their ideological boundaries to the extent that new "formations and sensations" of thought, experience and awareness will be necessary. New horizons will fill gaps that middle classes will soon realize, as life becomes incredibly easy and successful. However, this still will not answer the major "why" questions of existence. Just as society went "inward" relative to mind control and drug experiences in the '60s, the world will now move to "ultra-outside" to generate stimulative attention to the equation of life which we have not yet solved. The world will seek "new paradigms of the universe" to occupy its time and use as raw data to continue searching for "itself."

6. Finally, cultures all over this planet will be forced, by media, economics, ecological issues, and sheer numbers, to interact in forms of closeness which have never in history been experienced interculturally. Unification will be a temporary result, but the human mind's need to differentiate itself from itself and from other selves, will produce tension and conflict. This "anxiety" will happen between semi-merged cultures, that cannot be resolved by isolation, limited military muscle flexing, and formalized "legal agreements." Cooperative efforts fortunately, will develop to unite different peoples against a "third party," and eternal "enemy" or common challenge—which is the vast wilderness of the universal unknown in the frontier of outer space.

In all these situations, the world as we know it now will change drastically, just as it changed with the discoveries of the West, the atom, electricity, the computer, oil, etc. There are dangers, of course, in the many directions this revolution will take. There is opportunity to change ourselves, our outmoded and distinctive beliefs, and a window of stimulation to correct personal and cultural mistakes which have been transplanted through the ages by "ritualized compulsions" and traditions. We have a chance, one more time, to provide leadership for a universally peaceful, compassionate, understanding, cooperative and sane world, if we realize the massive shift in total universal energy that will occur in the very near future. We must also realize that this "disruption in balance" will give everyone a safe and honorable "way out" of the negative images and "systems" we have allowed to control our lives. The future will let us "change our minds" and reconceptualize priorities, to fill the enormous gap in cultural patterning and ideologic thinking that will emerge concurrent with comprehensive space exploration and settlement. We will, in concert, have the opportunity to:

1. understand the gross destructiveness of ego and culture-centric "values" which limit the potential of beings to "be";

2. halt the stupidity of discrimination which forms artificial categories of "nothingness," with exclusionary actions and attitudes that rob everyone of creative talents, ideas, and love we can all share;

3. work cooperatively with former "enemies" to realize we are the same, and have identical fears and interests for survival, significance, autonomy, freedom, and interdependent caring;

4. work internationally to explore the depths of human feeling, compassion, awareness, cognitive ability and spirituality, to elevate the human race to a level of meaningfulness and quality of experience never known by any previous civilization.

We must help the less fortunate, reduce irrelevant anxieties, destroy all destructive potentials of man and womankind, heal the sick and suffering, provide meaningful existence to the aged, nurture children in a reasonable and healthy way, eliminate crime and social destruction, cure mental illness, and eliminate hunger and pain everywhere.

Peace!